Hurt Without Hate

The Transforming Power of Forgiveness

By Tina Hodges

Cartoon Illustrations by David Whisson

Photography by Alison Johnson

Cover Graphics by Laura Jane Craig

Tina Hodges

tina@lovef1rst.com

LoveF1rst Publishing

www.lovef1rst.com

"As a result of using these principles I now have self worth. I no longer feel condemned. I've found that it's easier to forgive and not judge. I can process things better and I can receive and give help now without feeling pride. I sleep better and my past hurts don't replay in my head. Where I used to believe 'I can't' I now see that 'I can' and my burden is now light."

LC, mother of six lively children,
Sheffield UK

"Tina has a wide range of experience and knowledge in healing and wholeness and has seen many people set free from life controlling behaviours and patterns. She is great to work with and we have benefitted from her input into our ministries working with the vulnerable and the marginalised. We look forward to continued opportunities to work together in the future."

Andy Niblock, Team Leader,
Restore Ministries, St Thomas' Church Philadelphia

"Tina is a faithful servant of the sovereign God. It has been my experience that Tina listens diligently to the voice of God, and is a valiant, courageous, industrious, sensitive and caring, full-on woman of God."

TLA, UK

Dedication

I dedicate this book to my faithful Mum and Dad,
my delightful husband, Jasper,
and my wonderful daughters, Kitty and Loti.

Also, to my amazing God, Father, Son, and Holy Spirit.

Finally, this book is also dedicated to anyone who wishes
forgiveness as a lifestyle and has embarked on this journey.
May God's blessings be upon you in every way as you choose
this precious journey which so embodies God's nature.

Acknowledgments

I want to thank:

- ♥ **God**, my loving Father, for His belief in me, patience with me, and steadfast love, which is new every morning! Amazing!
- ♥ **Jesus**, for His love-without-strings, full and hearty acceptance, and whole-hearted sacrifice; for His call on my life to declare His name, His power, and love.
- ♥ **The Holy Spirit**, for the beautiful sweetness and amazing comfort of His fellowship, His mentoring of me, and His wisdom and gentleness with me.
- ♥ **Jasper**, my beloved gift of husband—the man beyond my wildest dreams, who has encouraged me in sharing my stories.
- ♥ **Kitty**, my eldest daughter, for her patient editing of this, my first attempt at writing.
- ♥ **Loti**, my youngest, for her patience in looking after me whilst I wrote this recovering from an operation.
- ♥ **David Whisson** for his patience with my vivid imagination and his creating the cartoons, which have added so much to this book.
- ♥ **All who patiently came alongside me** through my earlier life to encourage and uphold me, especially during my "messy years."
- ♥ **The heroes of my faith**—especially the overcomers: Martin Luther King, Corrie Ten Boom, Vanya,

David Wilkerson, George Verwer, C.S. Lewis, Bill Johnson, John G Lake, William Branham, Katherine Kuhlman, etc.!

- **The leaders of St Thomas' Philadelphia and The Order of Mission** for their inspiration, support, and guidance as I have transitioned in ministry.
- **Donna Kozik** who encouraged me that a book can be written quickly with integrity.
- **My fellow workers** who have a heart for wholeness and healing for all—that we may "spur one another on with love."

About the Author

Tina currently resides in Sheffield, UK, with her husband, and has two beautiful, grown-up children.

She is ordained and describes herself primarily as a spiritual advocate. In her previous career she was a Nursing Matron.

Tina's passions include watching action films, writing, painting (when she's on holiday!), bringing order and beauty from chaos, song writing, and enjoying lovely meals with friends.

Tina heads up a non-profit ministry called LoveF1rst, which seeks to "Empower People to Find Freedom and Wholeness Through Love."

Tina writes literature, gives talks, and runs seminars on a wide variety of topics that help people become more emotionally and spiritually free, including Overcoming Fear, Eliminating Stress, Learning to Love Ourselves and Learning to Forgive, etc.

Some of these resources for either the individual or groups and are available through her website (as are her free e-courses).

See www.lovef1rst.com for more details.

Contents

Introduction

Is This Book for You?

Pain is inevitable. Suffering is optional.

~ M. Kathleen Casey

Have you ever had someone say to you, "I'm sorry to hear that but you've got to forgive!"? And then you wanted to shout at them for their lack of understanding and empathy?

Hearing the words "you've got to forgive" can cause our hearts to really sink if we're still affected by the pain and injustice caused. We can feel others haven't got a *clue* about the enormity of the pain we feel and want to react with "but they did this to me!"

Where is the sense of justice in "just forgiving" when we're consumed by a wrong that has been done to us or someone we love?

Hurt Without Hate is my journey in learning to forgive—and boy, do I wish I'd known what I know now 20 years ago! I would have saved myself a great deal of heartache.

What Is Unique About This Book?

Forgiveness in essence is a journey in healing, and many are helped with counseling or psychotherapy—though this is not the route I took.

My journey in forgiveness, and consequently healing, has been one of ***applying spiritual truths as God has shown me them.*** As I have done so, things have changed in my spirit and emotions, and my physical health has improved also. My transformation is what gives me the confidence to share what I have learnt firsthand—the power of God/love at work in my life.

I'll guide you through the steps I've taken and try to translate for you some of the things you may be going through. Be encouraged that others who have followed these steps have found a new freedom themselves. Not only that, but their faith and joy in life have increased.

I have used spiritual principles because I've always wanted to know the truth. Later, I became a Christian—but even if you do not share my beliefs, I hope you will find something useful in what I share.

You can substitute love where I mention God, if that helps you. In fact, my journey with God started as I came toward the warmth of God's love, long before I really knew Him personally. Forgiveness is the utmost form of love that we can show ourselves, and I haven't always felt love near.

Where it All Began

From an early age I either experienced or observed abuses or injustices of many kinds and, as a child with increasing fear, felt powerless to do anything about them. Everything I observed: the programmes and "soaps" I watched on TV; people's experiences as they shared them of being victims; what I saw with my own eyes—these all showed me that life wasn't fair!

One thing built upon another and, not knowing how to handle the pain or injustice I felt, things just festered and grew in the dark. I grew even more sore and less joyful, and anger and frustration grew. I could trust no one; I was suspicious of everyone, and my sense of being powerless to do anything constructive reached an alarming peak.

Sometime in the process I discovered

that yes, I was hurt and reacted to that hurt, but what held me captive FOR SO LONG, was what I went on to believe because of the different HURTS (ultimately what I did—or didn't do—about my circumstances).

So what prompted the change? It has to be said: love.

Love crept into my life in different disguises and, whilst I did not see it at the time, it is what softened my heart, opened the door to hope, and finally led me into freedom to forgive God, others, and myself.

Making Sense of the Hurts

Is it Me?

You see pain imprisons us and when we're in pain we try and find the reasoning behind it. Is it me? Did I do something wrong?

These are the questions I asked when my second miscarriage came after a temper outburst on my part.

I was a fat child, and we were poor. That meant I stuck out at school in many ways—which often made me the butt of people's jokes, teasing, and bullying. I learnt to lie out of fear of being punished. And I had heard that "all liars go to hell." Maybe this was it.

Is it Others?

I didn't like others very much because they could be cruel and horrible—so maybe the problem was them, I thought. I lived in storybooks as a child, and those that caught my interest the most were those where there was a hero who "paid back evil for evil" or overcame stupendous odds—the ones where the hero/heroine had the last laugh after being treated cruelly by someone who was just "bad."

And then there were the authority figures in my life. From an early age, I realised that not all authority figures get it right, and some abused the authority they had—including the paedophile who abused me from the ages of 4 to 9. I still remember his leering face trying to entice me out from behind a chair where I was hiding to get away from him.

School was a place I had to survive. Bullying was everywhere, and adults seemed helpless to do anything about it. In fact the teachers were as bad as the kids, often sarcastic and teasing, unjust and unfair. I have no doubt that certain abusive teachers would have been sacked if they were teaching today, but in those days, it seemed that accountability was absent.

Is it God?

In Sunday school I came across stories and heroes that I learnt to look up to—but oh, they were so perfect! I would dream about being like them, but with the strong negative feelings I carried, the bad things that happened to me that made me feel dirty and bad, I believed the mirror was already broken and that such things could not be restored. I was Humpty Dumpty, or so I thought.

Surely God could have done something about my circumstances if He really cared. Why didn't He?

Surely if He is real, He would want to show it and rescue those who were unjustly treated?

He didn't come and rescue me in any way I could recognise, so I believed He didn't care. That made it easy to not care about Him.

Is it My Circumstances?

Like I said, we were poor growing up. Family benefits were not the same back then and what made us poorer was our isolation from others.

Part of the reason I had greasy hair was because we had to use washing-up liquid on our hair when money ran out because we had no shampoo.

I still remember my mum coming home from work with toilet tissue stuffed down her already ample front because we had none! At a younger age I'd learnt to appreciate the "TV times" over general newspapers because they made for softer toilet tissue! Visiting people who had such things as Andrex was a treat!!

When we had food treats (one family in particular befriended us in my younger years) I would stuff myself as much as possible with gateau or whatever, as I wasn't sure when the next treats would be.

So maybe our poverty was to blame for everything.

Is it "the Devil"?

Horror films gripped me as a child—both with horror and interest. It seemed that evil was stronger than good, and certainly that had been my experience.

Because fear was so ingrained in me, being bullied was a common experience, and injustice was all around me. Surely life was to be endured. "The Good Life" was really a dream and "The Real Life" was tainted and broken. I became superstitious out of fear, not knowing how controlling my feelings were becoming. I'm sorry to say that I was suicidal, too—and dreaming of how and when to kill myself was a common sordid occupation. I would dream of how those who had hurt me would turn up at my funeral repentant and wishing they'd treated me nicer! Whilst being suicidal started out quite mild, it became a serious problem when as teenager I became quietly depressed.

So was I to blame for it all? Was it due to my circumstances or other people? Or God? Or the Devil? Well, it would be nice if I could answer that simply, but I cannot. Life is not so black and white. Certainly some of these factors contributed to my becoming bitter and not knowing how to forgive. But so did a lack of protection, love, boundaries, support, encouragement, etc.

I'm guessing the same is true for you.

All this is now a long time ago, and I often say "when we know better, we do better."

Both those who hurt me and I have learnt a lot. Many are different people today, just as confused and disappointed that such things were part of our lives.

But what I would say is that "most people do the best they can with the knowledge they have at the time." I've met few really evil people. Most of us who need forgiving are just ordinary people who often mess up and try and learn from our mistakes.

If most people are doing the best they can with the knowledge they've got, ourselves included, then surely we should be a bit more merciful and kind when they mess up? That *includes ourselves!* The person I have found hardest to forgive in my life has actually been myself.

Of course, there are those who do downright evil things. They know it, we know it, and we need to build firm boundaries so that they do not continue to hurt us or others.

Then there are those who not only hurt us but abuse us, and when people do things illegally, no matter whether or not we forgive them, they may need to be prosecuted and sentenced in order to protect others from the same hurt. Even in these circumstances we can learn to forgive—but why should we bother?

Well, when we harbor unforgiveness *we* are the ones who are affected. We lose out. In fact, the other person may not even know the depth of hurt they've caused or even be bothered.

If we don't forgive, however, it will affect us much more than we can know. Unforgiveness is like a poison that spreads in our heart and mind, and paralyses us until we can hardly move.

You see,we're made to love.

And we cannot love where unforgiveness leads to bitterness, because the end result of bitterness is hate.

We cannot hate someone *and* be fully able to love someone, including ourselves!

We can hate the action the person does and the effect it has on us but we cannot hate *him* without affecting our spiritual, our emotional, and even our physical health.

Chapter 1

Is True Forgiveness Possible?

Since becoming a Christian I've been a believer of the What You Feed Grows philosophy (the title of one of my first public talks). Ironically, because I didn't know what to do with my own emotional stuff, I left it to stew, not realising that I was allowing it to fester in the dark.

I've learnt that you can't bury live* negative emotion without it affecting your thoughts, beliefs, and perceptions. Like putting a summer wardrobe of clothes away all dirty, negative feelings "put away" without cleaning them up first means that everything will take on an odour of its own by the time you get it out again!

* Like a "live" wire: If we had an electric shock we'd feel a surge of heat internally. Likewise, issues that are active and still "live" feel similarly but are strong negative emotions.

Prompted to Change

Sometimes it's not until we're flat on our backs that we look up. We have to be fed up of being a certain way, or of having the same experiences again and again, to be open to change.

Positive change then happens when we challenge what we believe now with a superior belief — and act on it.

God and Revelation

It is human nature to try to live our lives with whatever resources we can most easily access. Trouble is, often we fail to recognise the invisible loving force out there who is wanting and willing us to succeed. Our access to this force (God) does not depend on how good we are, but how open we are. When I became a Christian I started asking for God's guidance in my thinking and decisions, and I knew my biggest joys when I saw and felt God guiding me. It made His love for me feel more real.

Whoever we are, whatever we've done, when something happens which catches our attention (good or bad) we are meant to take note of it and take a step back so that we have chance to think and ponder on it. If we're just pondering on our own, we can miss out on important revelation and keep going round in circles. But thinking with others and in particular, inviting God to be part of the process, we invite a wisdom beyond ourselves into our lives and then we find that we begin to change for the better as we apply what we see. As good things result, our beliefs and actions change even more. There has been an AMAZING change in my circumstances in life. Freedom and grace, measure after measure. All because I didn't just look inwards and outwards, but upwards (to God) as well.

These regular insights and 'course changes' have taught me so many things and brought me the freedom I needed. I know these truths first hand (deep in my 'knower') and I have also had the privilege of helping others and being alongside those who have also found freedom as they have applied the same principles I learnt.

All things are possible for those who believe.
~ Jesus Christ (Mark 9:23)

You must do the things you think you cannot do.
~ Eleanor Roosevelt

Everyone thinks of changing the world, but no one thinks of changing himself.
~ Leo Tolstoy

Greatness is not in where we stand, but in what direction we are moving. We must sail sometimes with the wind and sometimes against it — but sail we must and not drift, nor lie at anchor.
~ Oliver Wendell Holmes

Prompted to Question

The question is not whether we will be extremists, but what kind of extremists we will be.... The nation and the world are in dire need of creative extremists.
~ Martin Luther King, Jr.

Like me, have you ever questioned God about the injustices you see around you?

Have you ever asked Him about pain and suffering — why many good people seem to have a harder time of it than others?

Have you ever noticed how people's reactions to hurt bring a variety of results, some becoming some bitter/cynical and never the same again? Others changing for the good?

Have you ever envied the resilience some people show to hurt and offence?

If you have, you're in good company. These things are what started my journey of questioning and pushing doors for answers.

Starting to Journey Positively

I've always loved books and films about overcoming the odds. I love heroes.

By the time I left school I was taught to obey without question, to do as I was told, and, most of all, to never to ask "why" (because to do so showed grave disrespect). Yet, I've discovered that God *loves* it when we come to Him with our questions, because He wants to answer us, and will answer us where we come humbly and are able to listen (although he does not always answer us in the way we expect — or even the way we would like!).

Despite the many opportunities to forgive those who have hurt me in my life, I often struggled to forgive because of my ignorance and my own emotional hurts. I know now that the more hurt we are, the harder it will be to forgive.

No more!! It doesn't have to stay that way.

Because God has brought me the freedom that comes with forgiving myself fully, others fully, and even God fully, I know that it is a matter of following each step until you get there. I can't contain the joy I've felt since I've let go!

In my story I hope you will see where your own forgiveness may be incomplete, and be inspired to finally get things sorted and take hold of the freedom that's yours.

The Effects of Emotional and Spiritual Overload

My parents separated when I was 3; a couple of new people in my life meant that I experienced various types of abuse as a child (physical, sexual, and verbal) from age 3 from different sources. I learnt that both strangers and supposed family were not to be trusted, and, being verbally and physically bullied from an early age, I found my life controlled and lacking nurture.

By the time I was a teenager I had learnt to fight to survive school and life in general; I comfort ate and I battled with a very low self-esteem and suicidal thoughts for most of my growing years.

During the second year of my nursing training I was diagnosed with rheumatoid arthritis and told I'd probably be in a wheelchair in five years' time.

Despite this I married, and in my twenties I suffered two miscarriages, a flare-up in the rheumatoid arthritis, which left me registered disabled for two years, and the disappointment of giving up my role as Matron in a nursing home among patients I loved.

Two years later I nearly died three times following a serious car accident in the United States (precipitated by a 17-year-old driver on the wrong side of the road).

More recently (in 2004) a marriage breakdown after eighteen years broke my heart and shook my ability to trust both men and women.

But I am not alone, and many people suffer like this or worse, on their own, often thinking like I did: that they must have done something wrong to have had such things happen to them.

Before I came to know God, I accepted all the stuff inside my head and what had happened to me, and quietly fumed. It was only after I invited God into my life that the possibilities of change and life being different began to grow in me.

Let me encourage you to "marinate" yourself in the stories of your heroes of faith. Our hope comes from knowing that things can be different.

Before I came to faith I would have described myself as hopeless; I was often suicidal, always angry, and often low.

I also found that people (church people included) sometimes avoided me because they didn't know how to handle me. No small wonder — I was a tearful child and an angry teenager. Life wasn't fair, and it seeped out of me in different ways.

"Ignorance will rob us of what we could otherwise possess and use."

~ Howard Carter

People didn't know how to deal with me, especially if they had a more privileged experience growing up. I think they felt they needed to be "specialists" to come alongside and befriend me, qualified in some way, but actually *I was just very open and very grateful to anyone who showed me love and acceptance.*

Thankfully God used loving people to bless me like that as a teenager.

I was definitely somewhat "prickly" — no doubt — but looking back on things now, it's no wonder I was. The emotional pain I was struggling with showed even if I couldn't see it myself at the time.

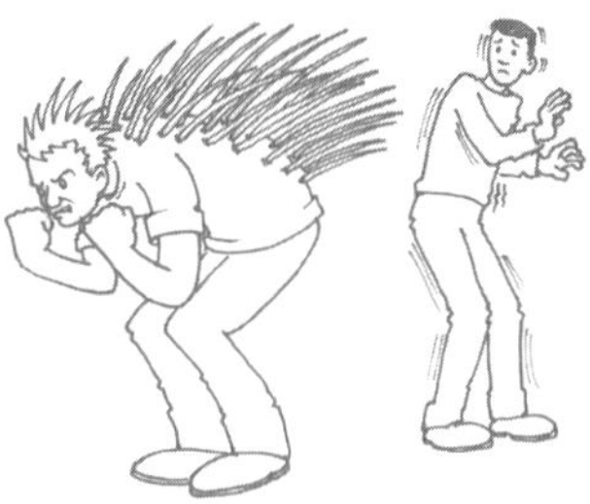

The truth is, I was just feeling unloved from the inside out, and any kind of love would have softened me. I comfort ate jam sandwiches galore and was nine stone by the time I was 9.

I felt great self-pity, as if the world owed me one; I learnt to fight at school in order to stand up for myself, was a force to be reckoned with by the time I reached 14, and learnt Judo from the age of 15 in order to be able to hold my own.

Not exactly the nun-like figure of gentleness I really longed to be!

A quick look back at how I handled my pain and I can see that nine out of ten times I chose to comfort my pain with food, escapism (books, films), burying my pain, and blowing up when I got angry — and lots of tears and wallowing "pity parties" on a regular basis.

What God Wants for Us

What God wants for us when we're in pain is for us to learn to love ourselves as God would have us loved.

You see, love — *healthy love — really is the antidote* to pain, anger, and every negative thing at work. Where I felt a deep and committed love as a child, I remained protected. Love does insulate us from all kinds of things like loneliness and blame.

It's amazing how much a human being can take if we have enough love, encouragement, and support. It's when we face life's difficulties feeling alone, confused, criticized, and abused that our pain turns inward first and then lashes out in a big way to someone or anyone who is around.

Instead of letting our past define us and dictate our future, through love we can dissolve the pain of the past, at last putting it to rest, and take up the life God wants us all to be living: a life of freedom and peace.

God loves it when we know how much He loves us. Because the key to our freedom spiritually and emotionally is to know God's love and let it transform us — to sunbathe and bask in God's love without fear, shame, or condemnation overshadowing us.

Handling Our Pain, Not God's Way

Comforting is the way we handle our pain without God. But I've learnt to handle my pain *with* God, and He showed me healthier ways of not only handling my pain, but re-introducing a much-needed and lacking element to it: His presence and perspective.

When we "love ourselves *as God would have us loved*" we're learning to go against the grain of bad habits, imprisoning life-styles, and negative thinking. We're choosing to believe and act with God Himself directing us with love.

Cherishing is learning to love ourselves as God would have us loved. Not pampering! That's for those who want their nails done or their hair cut! Pampering isn't a bad thing; that's just not what cherishing is. To be cherished is to be truly loved to pieces!

This journey will involve you learning to love yourself more and comfort yourself less.

What Do Comforting and Cherishing Look Like?

* Comforting aims for quick, often superficial relief of the issue without generally acknowledging or attempting to address the deeper issue.
* **Cherishing aims to address the deeper issue in a way that loves ourselves and others in a healthy way: mind, body, spirit.**

* Comforting doesn't solve the root problem but manages the symptoms only.
* **Cherishing addresses the root whilst allowing the symptoms to inform the way we do something, not allowing our symptoms to dictate the terms.**

* Comforters focus on the symptoms and not the wider picture.
* **Cherishers focus on the wider picture whilst also addressing de-stabilising factors (rest, sleep, good food, healthy boundaries, etc.).**

* Comforting has hidden consequences that are life-destroying.
* **Cherishing has hidden consequences that are life-giving.**

* Comforters find discipline hard and have negative nagging thoughts patterns (can't be done, not possible, never works…).

* **Cherishers can sacrifice more easily without feeling deprived, are open to ideas and thoughts that bless, and know that God can do anything in them and through them.**

So as we begin this journey in addressing the pain that is underneath our unforgiveness, I want you to really get this "loving yourself" firmly established. The extent to which you can take this onboard will have a direct effect on how quickly you are able to move forward to forgive.

In short, cherishing involves looking at where there are comforting roots and replacing them with love: addictions, bad habits (from anger to blaming yourself/ others), and self-sabotaging habits being treated with a loving/ cherishing mindset.

Unraveling what we believe about ourselves (unloving thoughts, beliefs, and actions) releases the stakes that keep us pinned down.

A spiritual law that few recognize is that ***our confession rules us. It is what we confess with our lips that really dominates our inner being.***

~ F.F. Bosworth

As you are able to be kind to yourself, can you encourage others to join you in loving and supporting you?

If so, you will target and process the pain that is holding your negative feelings and unforgiveness in place.

"I Once Was Comforted. Now I'm Cherished."

A disabled woman I knew, Emily, living at home, suffered with a bad pressure sore on her curved back for three years. The deep wound was dressed weekly by community nurses, but Emily was told that the sore would never be healed. Wounds were my speciality when I was nursing, so I approached the situation with confidence. By addressing each issue, the wound healed in three months, much to Emily's delight!

* A gauze "tyre" around the wound eliminated the intense pressure that was keeping it there.
* A swab and treatment for infection got rid of what was preventing the wound from healing.
* Nutritional supplements compensated for her tiny appetite and poor diet, and aiding skin healing.

Addressing and eliminating problems as they were identified resulted in complete healing within three months. Miracle working? To her it was, but in reality, it was merely problem solving — something I was taught to do as a nurse.

Food for Thought

When we make choices that only comfort, we are responding to our painful situation out of instinct, but the habits we establish are not usually life-giving for us (such as over-eating, over-drinking, over-working, over-spending, or even things like self harm) and they have a negative emotional/spiritual effect on us. Indeed, we become more and more constrained, and less able to live without our chosen comfort.

Freedom on the Menu

To become loved, accepted, and "made whole" does not depend on what we do, but on *knowing who we are*.

By experiencing God's love for me, I got a much better understanding of what I was and what I was created to be.

The power and strength I needed to overcome my situation was found as I developed a relationship with God. As my relationship with Him developed, I discovered that I no longer needed to carry the pain and burdens that were getting me down but could do a holy swap (divine exchange).

This is a process that we can all take: to exchange our "crap" experiences (excuse the language) for God's forgiveness, power, and a fresh start.

Where Love Should Operate in Life

1. Loving God
2. Loving Ourselves
3. Loving Others

What Does Love Look Like Spiritually and Emotionally?

Loving God

When we love God first, what happens is that we get to know God as Father*and realise that He loves us to bits. He delights in us (more than anyone you can imagine).

Condemnation and shame fall away as we experience unconditional love (love with no strings attached), mercy, and unfailing grace.

Judging ourselves and others falls away as His acceptance of us (as we are) drives accusing thoughts far from us, enabling us to accept ourselves, warts and all.

Fear disappears as we feel the acceptance, protection, and security of His love.

Control disappears as we surrender to His more wise ways and trust Him with our ultimate good.

Loving God is easy when we know and experience Him for who He is.

**And mother! Men and women are made in God's image, and both are needed to represent His whole image*

Loving Ourselves

When we love ourselves, we're kind to ourselves, especially when we make mistakes. We let ourselves off the hook easily.

We can laugh at ourselves and join in when others laugh with us without feeling insecure or picked on.

We have confidence in stepping forward with new ventures.

We have a healthy self-esteem and love ourselves, whatever size, shape, or age we are.

We have no need to push ourselves forward lest we miss out. We're confident the right things will come our way in God's timing.

We can separate ourselves from our mistakes.

Loving Others

When we love others we want the best for them.

We want to see them succeed and soar!

We're happy when they achieve great things, even when they outshine us.

We won't see them harm themselves without doing what we can to protect them.

We separate their mistakes or wrongdoings from them as people.

What an amazing effect love can have on us!

The Result of Right Choosing

Jesus shared the two most important rules for life:

1. Love God.

2. Love others as we love ourselves.

There is a highly important reason why it is wise to learn to love in this order (though I recognise we don't all get the choice to start with!). *If we love **others** first*, our love will be lacking in some way.

When we truly love ***God*** first, He ***always motivates*** us and empowers us to love others better. Our love changes the more we bring ourselves to God and soak in His love for us.

Loving Ourselves as God Would Have Us Do

Our love may be lacking when we do not learn also to love ourselves. (Often those most critical of others are critical also of themselves.)

Many of us will love as we have been loved, be it wholeheartedly, conditionally, sporadically, critically, or however. Also, *where we have lacked love, we will not have a genuine understanding of how to cherish ourselves as God would have us do.**

*This is not to say that those who have not received love cannot love, as God is a God of amazing grace and is the unseen force of grace at work in our lives, constantly willing us to succeed. However, Jesus did say "as you have received, freely give."

Jesus told us that we were to love others "as we love ourselves."

Yet the sad fact is that many of us are rubbish at loving ourselves as well as others.

Others of us love ourselves more than others. (A bit like grasping the soap in the bath, this love will elude us.)

Both of these fail to find the freedom that comes from true love.

God's love — divine love— is the highest form of love and is where we get both our inspiration and our power to love. As God's nature becomes "born" in us, our ability to love becomes transformed.

Never does the human soul appear so strong as when it forgoes revenge, and dares forgive an injury.

~ E.H. Chapin

Ignorance, sin, neglect, or selfishness? Take your pick. They all keep love out. It's only when we see the damage being done to ourselves when we're harboring "comforting" feelings like anger, resentment, vengeance, and hate that we can begin to see that hanging on to negativity turns us into what we're harboring.

You see, we can't truly love and hate a person at the same time. We can hate something he or she does, but hate cancels out love like a fire-blanket suffocates the fire.

God's Will for Us

God wants us to know ourselves as genuinely cherished. Being cherished involves our spirit coming into contact with love, grace, and truth, maybe for the very first time. The impact this has on our spiritual, emotional, and physical state is transforming and amazing. When we learn to cherish ourselves, we begin to know ourselves what it is to be truly cherished and find ourselves acting toward ourselves and others as God would have us do. Learning to cherish ourselves begins with choosing to listen to the voice of love and following God's lead.

When I was giving a talk on God being *for* us, one of the participants, Mark, responded in a lively way to the illustration I gave. He has given me permission to use this story. Here's the transcript for you to read for yourself:

Me: I have in my pocket a £10 note. Who wants it?

Mark: I'll have it.

Me: How did I know he'd say that? I'm going to give it to one of you, but first of all, let me do this. (I screw it up). Still want it?

Mark: I don't care; it's a £10 note. It'll still spend.

Me: Hang on. I haven't finished yet *(I stamp on it, I spit on it, and I rub it in my armpits.)* Still want it?

Mark: It'll still spend for me! You could put dog poo on it and I'd still have it.

Me: *(I smile.*) Many times in our lives we are spat upon, we're crumpled, we are dropped, we are muddied. Has this £10 note decreased in value? Despite the things that have happened to it. Are we decreased in value because of the things that are done to us? Are we of any less value? Absolutely *not!*

(Mark then interjects with the following story.)

Mark: When I was 16, I come out of care and had no way of supporting myself. I went in to the unemployment people and said I need some benefits, and they said, "Come back when you are 18."

I remember feeling so "oowh." Two years! How am I going to live until then? And I remember thinking, "God, what am I going to do?" and I remember looking through the papers, and I saw this job and basically it was working in B-wise uptown, and it was the most degrading job, and it was walking around with a billboard on advertising 3-piece suites. I remember feeling so degraded and so low and so stupid and so worthless. But then it gets worse. I got paid £10 a day and I got paid cash in hand. Then they asked me to put an owl suit on. So here I am walking around town and this owl suit got really hot and so I was walking around town and I decided to take the head off, walking with the head under my arm, feeling "oh God" and I remember someone came up and they kicked me, someone spat on me, and I saw these girls from a previous school that I went to and they were laughing, and I felt so humiliated and degraded. I remember feeling suicidal. I felt so worthless that I just felt like a piece of dog "poo" on the floor.

I remember walking, and my head was so down on the ground and I just felt worthless. I felt like there was nothing good in my life. It was not through any fault of my own it was more through circumstances really. I was doing the worst job, just to eat; council put me in a flat without checking out I had a benefit form or anything. I just did not know what to do.

I remember this guy came up to me. I was walking around, I must have looked just so down and depressed, and I just looked up and he put something in my hand. I remember instantly thinking, "Oh, it's a note, telling me how stupid I am." I honestly believed this was a note telling me I'm stupid, because I'm thick and I am stupid. I looked in my hand and he'd folded it up really small, and it was a £10 note, and I was astonished that someone should give me £10 when I am a worthless piece of poo, walking around with this board. And I remember walking around thinking, "Oh, who gave me that?" I couldn't see them, just to say thank you; somebody is valuing me. It was irrelevant that it was a £10 note. It was the fact that somebody on this planet had acknowledged that I existed and valued me as a person.

And when I tell that story, it is quite an emotional story, and I often pray for that person and I say, "Lord, remember that person who gave me the £10 note." I remember them and I thank God for them, because I think that was a point in my life where I could have quite easily killed myself because I felt that low.

(There was a long pause.)

Me: So for that story, Mark, you deserve the £10 note.

Mark: Thank you. *(He wiped his nose on it, at which we all fell about laughing!)*

Through partnering with God, Mark is now a different person, with a real heart for the hurting. He is married to Catherine and has five children (two from his marriage and three foster teenagers).

His life has God written all over it, and he leaves a testimony of God wherever he goes.

Chapter 2

The Process Involved

The difference between try and triumph is just a little "umph."
~ Bonnie Przybylski

Hear me when I say life *can* be different. Just because you carry hurt and pain today does not mean you always have to — in fact, God is absolutely passionate that you don't! And I'm standing right behind Him on that!

However, my well-meaning intentions alone will not get you free.

Lots of knowledge about this whole area of forgiveness alone will not get you free.

Putting on a face and pretending the hurt is not there will not make things better.

You may have a little thing to forgive, or you may have horrendous stuff to forgive. I am not being simplistic when I say that the process is the same. Like bereavement is a process to work through, the same is true for hurt and forgiveness. There may be particular tweaks that are applicable to your circumstances, but the process will always be the same.

Becoming free happens when we know the process, apply what is needed, and act upon it.

It starts with our desire to forgive. We must see the need to forgive and develop the capacity to do so if we want to know love and freedom. The person who is devoid of the power to forgive is devoid of the power to love.

Let me outline the process so you know what's coming.

The Spiritual and Emotional Process

1. Acknowledging What's Happened

First of all, you need to acknowledge the pain of what has happened and realise that God is on your side in it. You can't really start this process of forgiving without expressing trapped sorrow and pain — the injustice of it all, the pain we and others are left with as a consequence of being hurt etc.

Acknowledging the pain means we don't hide or pretend the pain doesn't exist. It's there. It happened. Life sucks.

Many people try to rush this process, but those I know who have tried to forgive and fail have hardly even paid lip service to this step.

Know that God validates your pain and others do, too. That means He's disappointed at what you suffered. It wasn't what He wanted for you, and He's angry about it, too!

It's what we then do with the pain that is the most important part of forgiveness. I'll come to this later.

2. **Knowing God Is *for* You:**

As you accept things that have happened, take hold of the knowledge that God is *for* you (even *if* you are fully or partly to blame). He's on your side.

Don't be hard on yourself! You have the power to change the pain or chaos caused by these things, as you get over the hurt:

All things are possible for those who believe.
~ Jesus (Mark 9:23)

For whatsoever from one place doth fall,
Is with the tide unto another brought:
For there is nothing lost, that may be found, if sought.
~ Edmund Spenser

3. **Taking One Day at a Time**

Don't be concerned about those who tell you it takes years to get over a hurt enough to forgive. It doesn't always. It can take years to finally let go enough and do what you need to do (or even weeks!), but *the key thing is to be listening to your mind, your will, and your emotions,* as well as being aware of the wider picture. I'll explain more later.

The degree and pace at which you find freedom actually depend on your passion to forgive and your ability to do *what* God says, *when* He says. (He knows us better than we know ourselves and understands the spiritual/emotional/physical interrelation, where we can be clueless!)

When my first marriage broke down, I knew I could not continue in ministry, stand up every week, and pronounce people's sins forgiven if I was burning with unforgiveness. It became a sink-or-swim decision, and I was determined to swim. I had the passion!

4. **Being Kind to Yourself.**

This is not about letting yourself off the hook, but about not allowing anyone to criticise or judge you while you process stuff.

You will be sore in the area you have been offended, but we're commanded in the Bible not to judge each other, because it is detrimental and undermines what God has created humankind for (mutual support and encouragement).

Well-meaning people will likely try to "sort you" with their advice. "You've got to forgive" can sound all very well, *but expressing the pain appropriately and giving it to God are the things that actually kick-start the process.* Until you are able to do that, then all the well-meaning advice in the world won't do a thing.

Do not allow any bullying thoughts you may have to put you down or get you down. In fact, listen only to what is positive and builds you up.

5. Trusting God

God alone knows your heart and how best to treat you during this time. Your close, accountable friends should be your advocates (like your cheerleaders!) who want the best for you. Be easy on them if they make mistakes, and listen most of all to what God says through His word to you. I'll share with you later more stories that have touched my heart about how gentle God really is.

I am certain that my own lack of wholeness contributed to some of the things that happened to me (especially as an adult), but God in His great love and mercy has brought restoration and healing in these areas of loss. I am now absolutely convinced that **the pivotal factor for change was in inviting God to work to redeem the loss, as I have journeyed in my forgiving.**

6. Partnering with the Holy Spirit in Everything

If God for us, who can be against us?

~ St. Paul (Romans 8:31)

Jesus gave us a wonderful promise and truth, and it is at our expense that we ignore it. He sends an advocate (helper, counsellor) to us, the Holy Spirit, who would be with us forever and lead us into all truth (John 15 and 16).

When we accept God's love, are sorry for our mistakes, and put our hand in God's hand, we become "born again," and the Holy Spirit makes Himself at home in us. Why? Amongst other things, because we're starting a journey of love — and He knows we need guidance in this journey of transformation, and who better than "God in us"?

Where we're living in partnership with God, the Holy Spirit depends on whether we listen and do whatever He tells us. Where we do, grace and freedom will follow, because God's wisdom always brings life.

7. Valuing Experience More than Information Alone

Don't dismiss the value of new experiences. Intellectual knowledge is not the way to truth. Surprised to hear me say that? Well, we all need to grow up, not get intellectually fat and flabby. There can be an over-emphasis on developing the intellect as a route to maturity. Knowing more about something doesn't change us, unless we use that knowledge to gain confidence to step out in new ways. Revelation is far more important than information.

8. Experiencing: Being Open, Teachable, Ready for Action

Knowledge without action is impotent. Experiencing something of truth first, and then afterward discovering the biblical backing for that thing can be possible as we trust the confirmation of the Holy Spirit to step out.

Living by faith and not by sight can deepen our ability to believe new thoughts we're hearing (the Holy Spirit), to trust this new thought enough to step out. Wisdom is knowing how to apply knowledge as we step out in faith, then heart knowledge (coming from our experience) will follow. We will find ourselves being led by love in the ways of Jesus.

What you know can keep you from what you need to know if you don't remain a novice. The moment I become an expert my theology becomes firm and rigid and it becomes a wineskin that is not ready for more or for increase. Child likeness is what keeps us in a place where we can continuously go from glory to glory. Faith is generated in the atmosphere of experiencing truth.

~ Bill Johnson

A Glimpse of God's Gentleness

One day I found myself on a prayer ministry team at a conference praying for someone I knew who had blessed me greatly in the past. As I started to pray, I literally saw a large frog leap out of his mouth. It was sudden shock to me! So much so, my insides curled at seeing it, as I'd never seen anything like that before!

I often get pictures for people as I pray, as that's how God often speaks to me. But this was different, and it got my attention big time. I continued to pray and saw two pictures.

The first was like a scene off the film *Goldfinger.* It was a naked woman who was covered in gold. The second picture was this guy I was praying for playing with a young woman.

Not knowing what to do with the first picture, I did my best to understand what I felt the other two pictures meant. I decided that God was just affirming his relationship with his wife and that he was to make sure he continued to have a strong element of fun with his wife.

He was happy to hear that and went home.

During the week that followed I kept coming across references to frogs in mouths being an indication of false prophets (those who claim to be speaking for God but are really not). This guy was a prophetic worship leader, so I wasn't sure what to do with what I'd had. I questioned whether I'd done the right thing.

I rang the woman who was ultimately responsible for prayer ministry at that conference, and she wasn't sure what to do either. Her only suggestion was that I might discuss this "frog" picture with his superiors. I was horrified at the prospect. What if I was wrong? I would feel awful. Not only that, but didn't Jesus deal with people face to face, not behind their backs? The last thing I wanted was to cause any damage to any of his relationships, and I am aware the hurtful effects of slander.

So I kept this situation in my heart, prayed about it, and asked God that if there was something He wanted me to say, that He would give me the opportunity to meet this man again.

Three months later I found myself at a different conference, and guess what? He was in the front row with his arms around a young lady who was definitely not the one I saw in my picture.

A-ha — the opportunity I prayed for! Not wanting to cause embarrassment, I asked God that if it was right, this man would be there at the end of the seminar and I would get the chance to speak with him alone.

Before the seminar was finished I was called upon to pray for someone, and, when I'd finished praying, I looked around at an almost-empty tent, except for this gentleman, who was sitting alone.

He was pleased to see me. I told him that he had been in my prayers since we last met (true!) and that I felt God had put something on my heart for him. I asked if he felt that he could hear me out. He said yes, so I shared what I felt God had told me.

In my prayer times God had shown me that this man had probems lusting after women, despite being married. I felt God say that He knew about this, but that if he still wanted the same level of anointing on his prophetic worship ministry that he had enjoyed that he had to "make a covenant with his eyes not to look lustfully at another woman." I said all this to him heart in mouth, fearful that I might be entirely wrong and possibly offending a really lovely man.

After sharing my heart, he looked somber and then confessed that even though he was in a men's accountable group, he secretly struggled with pornography, etc. since he was a teenager. Then he asked me if I would pray for him there and then.

I was somewhat humbled by the whole experience. I hadn't told him any of the details that had led me to pray for him for three months and was bewildered why God hadn't revealed this to one of his male friends instead of me.

The conclusion I came to?

God chose me to highlight this issue for him because God knew I had a high regard for this man. He knew I would speak the truth in love (one of God's amazing character traits) and do my utmost to be gentle and discerning.

...speaking the truth in love...

~ Ephesians 4:15

This is not the first incident of this kind I have had. I have now had many instances like this where God has shown me firsthand how kind and gentle we are to be regarding each other's weaknesses.

You see, ultimately, God is interested in restoration, not condemnation. He gives us chance after chance, wanting us to see His mercy and respond to it.

If we choose not to respond to gentle correction — to live outside of His protection — unfortunately we will reap the consequences.

God does want to destroy sin, but His aim is not to destroy the individual in the process if He can help it.

These various experiences have taught me that each of us as people is really precious to God. If He can get us to turn from hurting ourselves and others, He will.

Why do I share this?

Because I want you to know that God really is love and will be gentle with you through this process.

We see so much judgment in the church and the world, and some not-so-healthy habits because of it. People fall and, in our attempt to find and fix the problem, we can bruise and mistreat them for their mistakes. God is not like that.

You see, when something goes wrong we can automatically attribute blame to the person, yet God looks at our hearts and primarily blames our enemy for misleading, the one Jesus described as "the thief, who steals, kill and destroys" (John 10:10).

We may find it hard to separate people from what they have done wrong. God doesn't.

Just because you make mistakes doesn't mean you are one.
~ Unknown

Expect to Be Challenged

I've mentioned being open to new experiences — where you see a pattern and it feels like God/love knocking at your door, start to chat to Him and ask Him to guide you. Don't worry about mistakes; we all make them. If you're truly seeking love and freedom, He will know it and will give you every support He can to see you succeed.

Deep calls unto deep.... *~ Psalm 42:7*

Chapter 3

What We Believe Matters

We empower our beliefs. That is to say, what we focus on and believe in, we give power to.

Generally we don't think about why it is that we believe a thought, but that thought has come from somewhere. When we believe a thought, we believe the source of that thought, whether it's from God, the Enemy, or ourselves.

A lot of people have faith in themselves, but actually we're limited, so we're not doing the wisest thing to rely only on ourselves. We're not omnipotent; we can't do all things. That's God's job.

Uncovering the Lies

When it comes to forgiveness and healing, we have to recognise that we have believed things about ourselves that are wrong. We need to get rid of them.

To do this you've first got to challenge them, take captive every thought, and say, "Who goes there, friend or foe?" — in other words, are you of God, or of the Enemy?

If we can recognise that a thought is not of God, then we chuck it because we don't need it and it will only lead us astray. These thoughts give us names, such as "fat," "ugly," or "worthless," and God wants us to get rid of those old names so that He can give us new ones.

In the Old and New Testaments, people would give names to their kids relating to their character or things that they did (e.g., Dances with Wolves (I know, that one's been used!), Smiles a Lot, etc.).

God's name for us is who He's called us to be and who we are in Christ. We're called "Overcomer," "Precious," "Set Apart for God," and "Beautiful." They are all part of our inheritance as being a child of God.

But we have to get rid of our old names before we take hold of the new; we go through a sort of divorce — more than a divorce in fact. We cut them off *completely*, so we can believe in the positive thoughts about ourselves even in a hostile environment.

It can be hard to ditch old names if we're being reminded of them all the time by certain people. We may need a break away from certain people for a time to truly take on board our new names so that, when we are told damaging things, those things don't even touch us.

The Bible is very clear about how easily we can be influenced by hanging around with the wrong crowd. We shouldn't spend time with people who have the kind of things we're trying to get rid of, such as bitterness, anger, and hate. Not only will we become like them, but they will drag us down. We will need to a build a protective boundary. (I'll talk about how to do that later.)

Finding Our New Name

The way we find out our new name is to look up. We ask God, "What do you think of me?" and we listen and take what He says on board.

We know whether a thought is from our enemy because it will be negative. We know whether a thought is from ourselves because it will be predictable.

The thoughts that are from God are not only encouraging, but usually something we would not think of ourselves — something that is backed up by the Bible and our friends/advocates.

There's a song that says:

I will change your name
You shall no longer be called "wounded," "outcast," "lonely," or "afraid."
I will change your name your new name shall be "confident," "joyfulness," "overcoming one," "faithfulness," "friend of God," "one who seeks my face." (Anonymous)

Getting back to what we believe...

We Live What We Believe

If we believe that God heals today, but if we're not praying with sick people, we don't *really* believe it. Belief and action go together, like faith and works. When we believe differently, we live differently.

When Peter stepped out of the boat onto the water, his belief in Jesus kept him on the surface. It was only when he took his eyes off Jesus and noticed all the reasons why he shouldn't be walking on water, such as the huge waves, that he started to sink.

He cried out, "Lord, help me," and Jesus grabbed him. But instead of saying "Well done. Look how far you came!" Jesus said, "Why did you doubt?"

That may seem a bit harsh (after all, which one of us can walk on water?!), but the disciples were living with Jesus and seeing God's power at work every day.

Believing When it Really Counts

When God called us to Sheffield, I wanted to be accountable to some folks. I travelled up one day to meet some people from the church so they could listen to my story and help me decide if they thought God was really calling me there.

I drove up the night before, and I talked to God on the journey up, asking Him "How am I going to live? What am I going to live off?" because I was giving up my house and my income for the first time ever.

I'd always had someone to rely on financially, whether it was me or someone else. What I felt God was asking me to do was new to me, and then I saw a Mini (a car) in the hard shoulder of the motorway, broken down. It reminded me of a painful time in my youth when we couldn't afford to fix our car. We had to let it be scrapped and spent six months travelling around by moped and bicycles in all weathers.

Seeing the Mini raised in me the pain of the poverty we had at that time. It was a horrible time, worrying about money and having to "make do." In the end we bought a brand-new Mini on credit because we couldn't cope with it anymore. Seeing the Mini now reminded me of the difficult time we had, and I said to God, "Lord, I don't know if I can do it. I want to do it, but just the thought of it is so painful."

Immediately, my radio came on supernaturally and a song came on:

"All power is given in Jesus' name
In earth and heaven in Jesus' name
In Jesus' name I come to you
To share his power as He told me to.
Freely, freely you have received
Freely, freely give
Go in my name and because you believe
Others will know that I live."

God was just saying "I'm with you now. I'm giving you power this time. I'm sending you. I'm going to equip you, so FEAR NOT!"

I felt like heaven was behind me, and it gave me the "shove" I needed to step out in faith and live (as I did) for a year and a half "by faith," relying on God for every little thing we needed.

I must say, it was the *best* thing I ever did for my faith, as I leant on God so much and God showed Himself so faithful in providing all our needs, that my faith and confidence in Him grew immensely.

So, a bit like Jesus was saying "Keep your eyes on me, Peter, and you won't sink," God was saying to me at that time "You're stepping into new territory, but you're not going back to that place because I'm with you and I will provide."

Chapter 4

Friend or Foe?

Advocate or accuser — which do we want?

Bob's Advocate

Well that was most definitely a new experience for me today: sitting in that courtroom. And why do they still wear all that stuff — I mean grown men and women with white curly wigs on their heads and black flowing robes swishing this way and that with every forceful movement as they make their point?

Yes, it was very different, sitting there in that public gallery supporting old Bob in his hour of need.

I felt quite helpless. I wanted to help him, but I felt, well, unable to really. There he was, in that box looking like little boy lost. If ever anyone needed someone to uphold him, it was Bob.

And then it dawned on me: There was someone there to help him. His Counsellor.

There he was standing alongside him, his advocate, someone who would support and defend his cause, someone who would speak up for him, someone who has got to know Bob and was working for his best.

Bob had to face his problem alright and deal with them, there's no getting round that — but he didn't have to do it on his own. No, he didn't have to do it on his own.

How nice it would be if we all had our own advocate? They would definitely come in useful.

What's that, Lord? I already have one...? I don't have to stand on my own either?

Boy, if I went to court with all my problems and issues that I've been struggling with I'd need more than Perry Mason or Kavanah Q.C.!

Why didn't I realise it? I have the best advocate that there is: it's you, Lord. You're my advocate!

Supporting, defending, and upholding me, not because the law says so — oh no, it's because of your love and compassion, and that's not some excuse for me to do just what I want, because that same love is also there to gently correct me, too, and help me along the right path.

Hmm, here's a question, Lord: If your word tells me that I'm to be like Jesus, and that's some tall order, then are you telling me that I'm to be an advocate, too?

I think the words of John McEnroe come to mind now: "You can't be serious!"

You are?

Okay, seriously, do you want me to stand alongside others who are hurting?

Can I help those who are stuck?

Can I come alongside them and, through your spirit, help them to see a way forward?

Me, an advocate? I don't know, Lord; it's a tall order.

Possible, of course it is, but I'm only human.

I mean, when Bob told me what he'd done, it brought back some of my own difficulties that you know I'm still dealing with. But I did stand with him. I did support him. Yes, I spoke up for him and did what I was able to do.

You know what, Lord? If I could, with your help, become — and don't think I'm silly here — if I could become a kind of a mini Jesus, if I could get my attitude right then maybe, just maybe, I could, with your help, become for others what you have become for me: an advocate.

By the way, Lord, do I get to wear a wig?

My friend Paul wrote this sketch. Humour is one of the things that come as standard with Paul, but the thing I like about this monologue is that he sums up some of the processing we might go through as we aim to be an advocate for another.

What Is an Advocate?

"I'll be there for you" go the words of one of my favourite TV series soundtrack.

An advocate is someone who is there *for* us. On our side. Biased toward us. Wishing us to succeed.

Someone who is our accuser is definitely *against* us. "Out to get" us. Not wanting us to succeed.

We need the support and encouragement of those who are *for* us — who are our advocates — so we can be guided by them instead of being influenced by those who just accuse us, judge us, reject us, or criticize us.

Unhelpful Thoughts

I'm not just talking about people who accuse us, reject, criticize, or judge us, but our thoughts also. We need to fall out with those kinds of thoughts — and "send them packing."

We do need to be prepared to check out the thoughts we get and try to categorise them into friend or foe (enemy).

We'll find that easiest to do when we (or others) notice them.

What to Do with Unwanted Thoughts

If they regularly come up with a "live negative emotion," and the feeling seems out of proportion to the event, then there's some healing or forgiveness needed. There's stuff there that we haven't let go of or processed properly (maybe for good reason, or we didn't know better).

When I first noticed these, I "managed" them and tried to "put on a front" and pretend that they didn't exist.

I've also been through phases when I felt that expressing them whenever they cropped up was the right thing to do — until people around me started getting sore!

Finally, I learned a past/present/future approach, which I'd like to share.

Past

I'd get into the habit of asking God where in the past this unwanted thought and emotion came from. Sometimes I'd just be reminded of the trigger factor in the present, but when

I prayed about it enough, I found that God started to give me answers. Not often during my prayer time, but patterns would emerge or coincidences would happen that would trigger a thought in me and lead me to the answer.

I remember once asking God the root of my self-bitterness. During that time I was at a conference where I'd taken two friends along for them to be blessed. I was disappointed when I realised that, because of my schedule, they would miss out on some really good prayer ministry, and my disappointment showed. After a brief conversation, the speaker thought I was disappointed about me not receiving ministry (which was not the case). He obviously felt somewhat guilty, as he was exhausted and already overstretched, and misinterpreted my actions as my own disappointment. He proceeded to look at me several times during his next seminar while referring to his inability to do "everything" and respond to every demand that came his way.

I was stunned to be misinterpreted and embarrassed that he then referred to the matter publicly in a veiled way. He is a really lovely man, and I have a great respect for him, and I chose not to get offended, but then I felt like an amazing thing happened. God showed me the root of my self- bitterness as public humiliation. Coincidentally, this chap looks very like the one who used to shame me publicly – bingo! I found the root of the shame, and I was able to give it to God (see later chapters for details of how it can be done). I could say I wish I hadn't been misunderstood, as it may not have done my reputation much good, but God chose to use it to help me out after all!

I needn't have worried about my friends either. They both got some one-to-one time before we all left.

God can choose all kinds of things to speak through if we're looking for answers earnestly.

Faith is courage; it is creative while despair is always destructive.

~ David S. Muzzey

It's not what you look at that matters; it's what you see.
~ Henry David Thoreau

Present

In the present, I've learnt to recognise when an unhelpful thought surfaces because it unsettles me, causing my emotions to become more exaggerated than usual.

When we're affected by unwanted thoughts, we always have a choice whether to believe them or not. When we believe them, we empower them. The more we learn about God, ourselves, and love, the more we understand that God is love and that to overcome these thoughts we need to become aware that we have an enemy that likes to plant thoughts in us as if they are our own. We need to reject these accusing thoughts in favour of the loving ones.

When we focus on these insecurities we start to believe them and agree with them until we eventually become like them!

At any point during the process we can turn things around.

King Saul would try to turn things around by distraction — listening to some calming music. He even had David play for him. Distraction is still a good temporary way to calm down (counting to ten, watching a film, etc.), but we need to do more than that.

What is the key to overcoming unwanted thoughts in the present?

I've learnt to invite God into the chaos of the present moment and ask Him to come and show me the way to Him, even while I'm still feeling smelly and affected by what I or others have said and done.

God specializes in bringing order

out of chaos, and nothing can separate us from His love, which can reach us everywhere.

There is no place inside or outside of us that we cannot invite God/love to come.

Can anything ever separate us from Christ's love? Does it mean he no longer loves us if we have trouble or calamity, or are persecuted, or hungry, or destitute, or in danger, or threatened with death? ...No, despite all these things, overwhelming victory is ours through Christ, who loved us.

And I am convinced that nothing can ever separate us from God's love. Neither death nor life, neither angels nor demons, neither our fears for today nor our worries about tomorrow—not even the powers of hell can separate us from God's love. No power in the sky above or in the earth below—indeed, nothing in all creation will ever be able to separate us from the love of God that is revealed in Christ Jesus our Lord.

~ Romans 8:35, 37–39 NLT

God moves surprisingly quickly when we do this. He is so thrilled that we're turning to Him in our mess that He's like the prodigal son's father who comes rushing out to meet us and throw His arms around us.

Usually I'm then led to kick those thoughts out and find a truth that God wants to share with me to keep it out — like the story I shared in the last chapter about fear of poverty, with how God used the truths in that song to speak to me His "now" word to give me what I needed to hang onto.

Why Is Validation/Sympathy Important?

Because validating our hurts is part of the process of healing, and this was the thing that was most lacking in my own journey — mostly because I rarely opened up and shared with others out of fear of their response.

What Is Validation?

Validation is like sympathy where our pain and our bruised spirit, thoughts, and feelings are told they are "okay" and "justified," given what has happened. They are affirmed. It's what those with empathy do naturally:

> "You poor thing."
>
> "Really? That's awful!"
>
> "I would be angry, too!"
>
> "That sucks!"

And when we know God well, we can validate what God would say:

> "God isn't happy that happened to you."
>
> "God's angry about that, too!"
>
> "God is weeping, too. That was not supposed to happen."

Many times in my journey I have heard the supportive validation of the Holy Spirit through my thoughts. In fact, my songwriting, which lifted off when I became a Christian, often contains validations and affirmations that I had heard God say, and singing them often helped keep my faith afloat.

Validation from the Holy Spirit can be heard through lots of different contexts and through different people — whether or not they know of your hurts.

Validation Comes Before Forgiveness

Like a gentle answer turns away anger (as the proverb says), so validation injects comfort into pain and anger, and can loosen stubborn unforgiveness.

Jesus sticking up for the woman caught in adultery who was going to be stoned was validation. The reason validation of our feelings is necessary for forgiveness is so that we know that someone understands and *cares.*

When someone understands and supports us, we can more easily let go of being hurt by someone, because our story has been heard and we have felt listened to.

Oftentimes when I work with others to help them forgive, they make progress really well once they realise their story and feelings are valid. They feel encouraged because they are heard and because they move into forgiveness more easily.

Shaping Our Future

When we have acted on truth (no matter how wobbly or fearful we are when we're doing it) we will affect our future positively.

Likewise, when we act on lies that we have come to believe, we will restrict our future in some way. The spiritual world is a remarkable thing. Instead of being an "added extra" to our human dimension, our decisions here affect our spirit, our emotions, our intellect, and our physical health.

Thinking positively is just not enough to change our future. As we *act* on our thoughts, we give power to the thoughts and the source of these thoughts as we demonstrate our belief in them — be they from a good source or a bad one!

Our future will be affected by what we act on now, in the present.

Who Are Our Advocates?

Our friends who support and encourage us, yes, but particularly those who have a hunger for truth and who don't settle for easy, comfortable lies.

The Holy Spirit is our ultimate advocate — our helper, friend, and counselor who not only speaks to our thoughts, but brings revelation where we seek it. The Holy Spirit is also like our satellite navigation guiding us as and when we think/act and speak (Romans 8:26–27).

God the Father is our advocate who set up the process by which we can be restored to relationship to Him:

For God loved the world so much that he gave his one and only Son, so that everyone who believes in him will not perish but have eternal life.

~ John 3:16 NLT

Jesus is our advocate.

Who will bring any charge against those whom God has chosen?

It is God who justifies. Who is he that condemns? Christ Jesus, who died—more than that, who was raised to life—is at the right hand of God and is also interceding for us.
~ Romans 8:33–34 NLT

With these important advocates being for us,
who cares about what others may say?!

Chapter 5

The Emotional and Spiritual Rollercoaster

Joyce Meyers says, *"It's torture to have hateful thoughts towards another person rolling around inside your head,"* and I agree.

When we're hurt and we have all that sort of stuff going on in our head, we want to get rid of it as soon as we can.

What I want to see happen for people is for them to go from being overwhelmed to overcoming. I love that quote from Winston Churchill that says, "If you're going through hell, keep going."

Another author said, "A bend in the road is not the end of the road unless you failed to make the turn." (Author Unknown)

This chapter is more of a first aid treatment — what to do if you're having a "live" emotion moment. Remember what live emotion is? It's the initial "*argh!*" feeling that kicks off an emotion, like a live wire.

When we're in live emotion, our objectivity is affected; emotion is conveyed in our voice, but not always as a clear emotion, so it messes up communication. People can hear the live emotion and think all kinds of things, like we're "against" them when we're not; we're just "live."

Be Careful of the Instant

The first thing to do is be careful what we say and do in live emotion, because we will usually regret it later as we gain more objectivity, as we hear all sides of the story, and as we calm down.

The Cherishing Process

A Problem Shared Is a Problem Halved

Some people can calm down just by spending time alone, but if they're in pain, it is better to share it, although God counts as someone we can share with.

Others just get more and more worked up as they go over why they're angry in their head. Advocates — accountable people — are life-savers for times like this, so that the hurt can just be unloaded.

If advocates offer advice we don't want to hear, we need to find someone else to talk to. We're not talking to them to ask for advice; we're talking to them to process things in our own head.

What I say to people is this: "I'm going to share this with you and I value anything you say, but that doesn't mean I'm going to do what you say."

Honouring My Pain *and* My Relationship with Love

I also make sure I don't mention any names, so as not to gossip or slander. I like the fridge magnet that says "Be kind to your children. They choose your nursing home!" Likewise, I've discovered that the person I'm unhappy with today may be a friend tomorrow and I want to ensure my heart stays right.

Most of us need to someone to talk to when we're in pain. It helps us process better.

We also need to cherish ourselves around such times by eating well and sleeping well, using remedies, and cherishing so we are at our physical best to be able to cope with the emotion.

The last part of first-aid treatment for live emotion is boundaries: We still need to feel protected and loved.

Godly Swap

Throughout our whole emotional and spiritual roller-coaster, God has already given us a solution: the divine exchange, where we exchange issues we no longer want for the happiness and freedom that can be ours with laying it down.

If we're Christians we do that at the cross. If we're not then we just lay it down and leave it. Even if we have to keep doing it until it stays "left."

I've known this divine exchange happens most effectively by giving it to Jesus, but many people can recognise where they need to let go of something and pick up something more life-giving instead.

Mercy for Mercy

The Bible tells us that mercy triumphs over judgment. This does not mean that we will draw the short straw — that we will be badly treated, left neglected, and then expected to show mercy.

We can be merciful because God has ways of making it up to us, if not in this world, then in the next. God's restoration and justice are so much better and greater than ours.

Recognising the Smellies

People being offended easily is evidence of unforgiveness toward someone (God, self, others) in their hearts.

We can find ourselves taking something personally and being hurt by what someone says. My choir mistress when I was young would sometimes announce to the choir "Someone's singing out of tune!" but I heard "Tina, you're singing out of tune!"

I obviously felt it was me just because my opinion of myself was low. The highlighted emotion is what offence feels like — like you *feel* it's to do with you.

Pastor Henry Wright, the founder of Be In Health Ministries (www.beinhealth.com) has outlined seven parts to bitterness.

He talks about bitterness as going from unforgiveness, to resentment, to retaliation, to anger and wrath, to hatred, to violence, to murder.

If we detect any of the above in our hearts (and most of us know what these feel like) then we still have some more working through forgiveness to do. The more on the list we identify with, the more serious it is that we take this job of forgiveness seriously!

These can be eliminated, but we cannot keep putting things off without it harming us and our other relationships.

I suggest that the doorway into unforgiveness starts with offence. Now, some offence is perfectly understandable (such as if someone runs over our dog). But other examples of our offence can reveal how easily we are offended and, therefore, the level of spiritual and emotional baggage we're carrying.

The following was a story of someone I read about (who shall remain nameless) who was an enthusiast for cars, Cadillacs mainly:

"... owned about 100 during his lifetime. But in the 1970s, the talk among car buffs was of a sleek Italian-made sports car called the Pantera (Panther in English) and...bought one. One day when he fancied a spin, the car would not start. ...took out a gun and shot it, twice or possibly three times."

This guy had obvious smellies. My guess is he hadn't a clue how to understand them, never mind get rid of them.

Here are some sound quotes that deserve more than a little reflection (to help spur you to forgive!):

"Anger is never without a reason, but seldom with a good one."

~ Benjamin Franklin

"Resentment is like taking poison and waiting for the other person to die."

~ Malachy McCourt

"In taking revenge, a man is but even with his enemy; but in passing it over, he is superior."

~ Sir Francis Bacon

"Something of vengeance I had tasted for the first time; as aromatic wine it seemed, on swallowing, warm and racy: its after-flavor, metallic and corroding, gave me a sensation as if I had been poisoned."

~ Charlotte Brontë

"Those who plot the destruction of others often perish in the attempt."

~ Thomas Moore

"Revenge converts a little right into a great wrong."

~ German proverb

"You cannot get ahead while you are getting even."

~ Dick Armey

"Revenge has no more quenching effect on emotions than salt water has on thirst."

~ Walter Weckler

"That old law about 'an eye for an eye' leaves everybody blind. The time is always right to do the right thing."

~ Martin Luther King, Jr.

"There is no revenge so complete as forgiveness."

~ Josh Billings

"Do not spread slanderous gossip among your people. Do not stand idly by when your neighbour's life is threatened. I am the Lord."

~ Leviticus 19:16

Ejecting Smelly Emotions

When I first recognised some of these things in me a long time ago, I recognised they were not of God. I'd read a Christian book about "crucifying the flesh" and recognised that I need to take them to the cross and crucify each one of them. In other words, they needed to die.

I may have wanted to keep my smellies at one time, but I didn't want to anymore. I wasn't even sure if it was possible to let go of those things, but God seemed to be leading me, and so I did. It was like literally nailing things to the cross. Jesus talks about dying daily to ourselves, and I see that as dying daily to those things that I don't want as well.

So we take them to the cross, we repent — in other words, we declare that we have changed our minds about something and don't want it anymore; we don't want to feel this way anymore — and then we leave them there.

It's best to speak out our thoughts at this stage. The things we say in our hearts are heard by God but, whilst our adversary can plant thoughts in our minds, he cannot read them. Letting him know his lies are known by us and that we kick them out in Jesus name is important.

We don't want to pick up our trash again, and we don't want to take it away with us because we are completely falling out with this stuff and never want them again.

I did this most effectively in 2004–2005, and managed to forgive and move on in what seemed a very painful and impossible situation. I spent a number of months putting my trash and pain down at the cross and trying to pick up God's grace in its place.

I found that the process is always longer when there is hurt that is deep, affects others, or is invalidated.

Judgment

Another "smelly" emotion is judgment. When we've been hurt and we're getting into unforgiveness, judgment can very easily come in through the door. We just think, "This person hurt me once. Therefore he's always like that," and we then develop a "holier than thou" attitude. He's a bad person in our eyes — and not only that, but we become aware of other splinters in his eye and we forget the flipping great plank in our own! Truth is, we all have blind spots and hurt people without intention. This is why forgiveness must be a lifestyle if we are going to stay afloat.

Judgment prevents us from seeing the good that lies beyond appearances.

~ Wayne Dyer

If we see things that need to change in others, that doesn't necessarily mean we should or need to point them out — unless we're seeking to forgive. (The Bible is very clear in stating that if someone has hurt you, you go and talk to them about it.)

To sit in judgment of those things which you perceive to be wrong or imperfect is to be one more person who is part of judgment, evil or imperfection.

~ Wayne Dyer

Blame

Raising conflicts is best not done in a blaming way (i.e., "You did this to me") because blame is another "smelly" thing; it makes us want to lay all the responsibility at someone else's feet for something that happened, even if there were things we may have done to make matters worse.

With blame we need to recognise where responsibility truly lies, and take our own responsibility before laying other blame elsewhere. That doesn't mean that we then have to beat ourselves up!

The wonderful thing is, as soon as we become aware of our part, take responsibility, and say we're truly sorry, we give it to God and He takes it straight off us!

If the cause of the hurt is primarily someone else's and we still feel like we're the ones to blame, we may have an "overactive guilt gland." Maybe we grew up in an environment where blame was common or people didn't take responsibility as they should have. Maybe saying sorry was seen as weak, or we feel so badly that we've got something wrong that admitting it "tips" us over the edge.

Ultimately, God knows what happened, and He knows our hearts. Where we're seeking revelation He will start to open the doors to understanding.

I am never a failure until I begin blaming others.
~ (Unknown)

A man can fail many times, but he isn't a failure until he begins to blame somebody else.
~ John Burroughs

Vengeance

Vengeance is the other "smelly" emotion. It's a bit like lust in the sense that it satisfies an immediate desire to do something destructive in order to get our own back. But it doesn't necessarily sort out the issue of justice long-term. When we take matters into our own hands, we show our lack of understanding of God's ways because we don't realise that actually, if we give our smellies to God let them go, He will sort out those things better than if we try to do so alone. In fact, if we choose our way of putting things right, God will step back and allow us to do it ourselves. He doesn't force us — but oh, His way is soooo much better!

We then don't end up taking smelly emotions on in our hearts. We don't want to stink, do we? I don't want to stink, especially from the inside out. I "sure" ly (!) don't!

He who seeks vengeance must dig two graves: one for his enemy and one for himself.

~ *Chinese proverb*

Beloved, do not avenge yourselves, but rather give place to wrath; for it is written, "Vengeance is Mine, I will repay," says the Lord.

~ *Romans 12:19*

The Spirit of the Lord GOD is *upon Me,*
Because the LORD has anointed Me
To preach good tidings to the poor;
He has sent Me to heal the brokenhearted,
To proclaim liberty to the captives,
And the opening of the prison to those who are *bound;*
To proclaim the acceptable year of the LORD,
And the day of vengeance of our God;
To comfort all who mourn

~ *Isaiah 61:1–2*

Hands Off!

Taking matters into our own hands also shows a lack of trust in God.

It can be understandable where we haven't known the presence and covering of God as we should have, but one sure way to get God's attention is to seek Him above everything, and search for the comfort and solutions that He already has for us.

It's one thing to tell God that you know He will take care of the issue of forgiveness, but that will only happen when we lay it down and *fully* take our hands off it.

Only then can He do something with it. If we still have an interest in it, then we haven't fully given it to Him. If we take it into our own hands, we disallow God to show His grace and restoration to us in that area.

Turning Around:
It's All About Him — "Metanoia"

In the Old Testament this word for repent meant a change of heart, but in the New Testament it means a change of mind. Ultimately, what metanoia is about is "His way, not my way."

When we recognise that something we're doing is lacking, we're far more open to God. We're far more open to learning a different way and taking hold of God's way of doing things instead of our own.

It's easy to hand things to God when we know He has our best interests at heart. He knows more about how we're made and what would happen with the choices we make. We can trust in Him more confidently.

Metanoia is no longer about me; it becomes all about Him. The thing about envy, jealousy, bitterness and judgment, and rejection is that all these things focus on "me."

Any attempt to get fairness in my life by "me" doing something, leading it my way can very easily make us independent and allow pride because we're trying to do things on our own strength instead of allowing God to come in and show us how to do things his way.

We can do things so much more in His strength than we can in ours. "I Did It My Way" is a sentiment that couldn't be more distant to what I'm talking about.

I'd much rather people sing at my funeral "She Did It God's Way!"

"I Once Was Blind, but Now I See"

The other part of metanoia is recognising our part in our own downfall — not by placing blame, but by realising that we couldn't see something before, we can see it now, and we're going to do something about it.

Fighting Truth Decay

Another thing about metanoia is we will always need to uncover a lie from the Enemy and replace it with God's truth. When we truly repent, we're desperate to see where we went wrong and most open to the Spirit's guidance in this.

Once we stop believing a lie we can start believing the truth. It may come to us the other way round — as revelation often does — but the important thing is that we recognise we've been mistaken, we've been duped, and we can do something about it by planting the truth in its rightful place!

This changes our allegiance — who we're relying on. God/love becomes the "solid rock on which we stand."

We're told in the Bible about renewing our minds: "Be transformed by the renewing of your mind."

Some of us can believe utter rubbish and not realise it, or, worse, we think it's okay. It does have an effect on us.

We have an allegiance to either God or the Enemy, and we need to make sure that all our allegiance is to God. God is love, and when we're relying on Him and His ways then we are going to reap a good, loving, and positive benefit.

Bitterness imprisons life; love releases it. Bitterness paralyzes life; love empowers it. Bitterness sours life; love sweetens it. Bitterness sickens life; love heals it. Bitterness blinds life; love anoints its eyes.

~ Harry Emerson Fosdick

"Forgive them, Father, for they know not what they do."

~ Jesus in Luke 23:34

If you forgive men their sins, your heavenly father will also forgive you. If you don't forgive others their sins, neither will your father forgive your sins.

~ Mark 11:25

Chapter 6

Stuff Happens

When you come to the end of your rope, tie a knot and hang on.
~ Franklin D. Roosevelt

Sometimes life sucks, and it's just not fair what happens to some people. But what's worse is the many lives I have seen battered and sabotaged by bitterness and unforgiveness, because the person in pain finds it hard to let go and move on unhindered after a hurt or loss.

The Bigger Injustice

The bigger injustice here is that not only have people been hurt once, but they continue to live devastated, unable to find peace and freedom because they lack the know-how of what to do with their pain and sense of injustice.

This is a great wrong. But good news! Hope, freedom, and peace do come when we learn to forgive.

If your heart is unsure of forgiving because your spirit is already exhausted from carrying hurt, don't despair. *This process should be light, not heavy, because you are ultimately in charge of*

it. You are in the driver's seat, and I will be encouraging you to listen to yourself as much as you listen to God. It is fundamentally important that you learn to be kind to yourself in the process — and not drive yourself to do more than you are able to do at one time.

I spent many years wishing I wasn't here because my emotional pain was so bad and I didn't know what to do with it. Partly that was because of various "assaults" that I had; partly that was because I was hard on myself (you guessed it: I found forgiving myself the hardest thing).

Getting Up, Not Giving Up

Being hard on ourselves is just what the enemy wants. Jesus was *full* of grace and mercy. He wants us to learn how to be loving and merciful to ourselves; it will be hard to be merciful to others where we are not including ourselves.

I used to pray, "Lord, take me now. I've had enough!" Seriously! *Not* a good thing, nor something I would recommend. I have learnt instead in recent years that God can renew and refresh our spirit, so when I have felt worn and feel I cannot go on, my prayer now when I'm facing a challenge is: "Lord, give me strength!"

Even youths will become weak and tired, and young men will fall in exhaustion. But those who trust in the Lord will find new strength. They will soar high on wings like eagles. They will run and not grow weary. They will walk and not faint.

~ Isaiah 40:30–31

Saints are sinners who kept on going.

~ Robert Louis Stevenson

Our greatest glory is not in never failing, but in rising up every time we fail.

~ Ralph Waldo Emerson

The Truth About Anger

Anger can be a positive emotion. However, only when we have fully conquered anger can it be fully positive.

True or false?

Angry people can just learn to control their anger. False.

I would have said I was the angriest person on earth at one time. I could shout, swear the wallpaper off the wall, and even hold my breath in a fit of rage! I thought it was normal, because many people I knew had a problem with anger. I thought it was just a matter of managing it and that I was just rubbish at doing so. Not true!

You see, underneath anger is often pain. Depending on the degree of emotional pain being felt, the harder it is to be able to "manage" it, especially when you're not given any tools to know how to deal with it.

Emotional pain that remains unprocessed is cumulative; that means each hurt builds on one another. If we get offended about little things and think that's okay and we *don't deal with the root, then our anger will keep deepening.*

True or false?

We can hide our anger and time will sort it all out.

False.

It is important that we acknowledge our pain and anger, because otherwise we bury these things alive and they will come back to bite us at some point.

Imagine an issue arising like a ticking timer being set to run. One ticking noise we can cope with. Then another issue and another timer. Two lots of ticking. Now imagine fifteen of these ticking timers going in the background. They would drive you nuts!

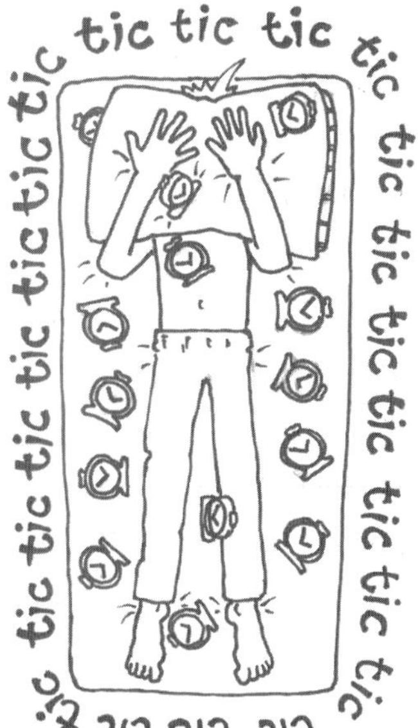

Unfortunately we can't throw all these things out because they're in us, but do you get the picture?

We have to address each ticking timer one by one, looking at why and when it started, then letting the anger go. (I'll show you how to do this in the next couple of chapters.)

True or false?

Being angry can prevent our healing.

True.

It's not about controlling anger. This can be really hard when the pain is deep, and we cannot do this without damaging ourselves when it has turned to rage.

But we can see things differently and thus not get angry in the same way.

Hope's Disappearing Act

We can lack hope over all our lives, or we can just have a couple of areas (the areas where we're still stuck) where hope has disappeared — where we feel that nothing will change or improve.

What does a hopeless life look and feel like?

- Life is forever broken and cannot be fixed.
- Nothing we do will make any difference.
- The factors that are constraining us are too strong for us to overcome.
- No colours are left in the world anymore. Everything seems grey.
- We've forgotten what joy is. Everything is tiring and a drain.

Hopelessness in our spirit is the result of failing to process the "bumps and bruises" on our spirit, with the result that we're left believing lies and living according to them.

Hope (or lack of) has everything to do with what we believe.

The sooner we can challenge the lies that we have believed with God's/love's truths, the better.

You should be careful about what you believe because "when you believe a lie you empower the liar."

~ Bill Johnson

What I would say is this: Just because life has knocked you down doesn't mean that you're a bad person, that God doesn't love you, or that you don't deserve better.

New Mercies as We Give Our All to God/Love

When my first marriage broke down I was devastated. He was my first love, and I had no strategy for what to do in such a situation.

But I threw myself onto God — hook, line, and sinker!

Feeling like a failure and unsure if I could trust enough to love again, it never occurred to me that God would have a delightful man in the background for me. I often say to my now-husband that he is not the man of my dreams (!) because I never even dreamed someone like him was there for me. He's a gift *beyond* my wildest dreams!

However, my hope grew one step at a time. God's assurance and others' assurance (with confirmation from the Bible/others) paved the way to my step-by-step restoration.

The thing about "new mercies," or new opportunities, is that we need to give up on that old thing, but not to give up without God. We give it up *to* God.

How We Give Our All to God/Love:

1. **Surrendering to God's ways:** "I don't know what to do with this mess, but *I give all this to you and ask you to lead me and guide me* instead. *You take over. You guide me every step of the way.*
2. **Metanoia —Spirit-led change of heart/mind:** *"Show me where I'm believing a lie, and tell me what the truth is."*
3. **Separating ourselves from lies, wrong beliefs, and actions:** *"Help me to separate myself from the lies I've been believing and the behaviours that aren't of you."*

4. **Looking to God/love for truth and gruidance:** *"Show me what to do."*

5. **Resisting the instant solutions:** ***"Don't let me be led astray*** by *anything that is not you."*

6. **Making life-embracing decisions:** *"Help me to choose life in all my actions."*

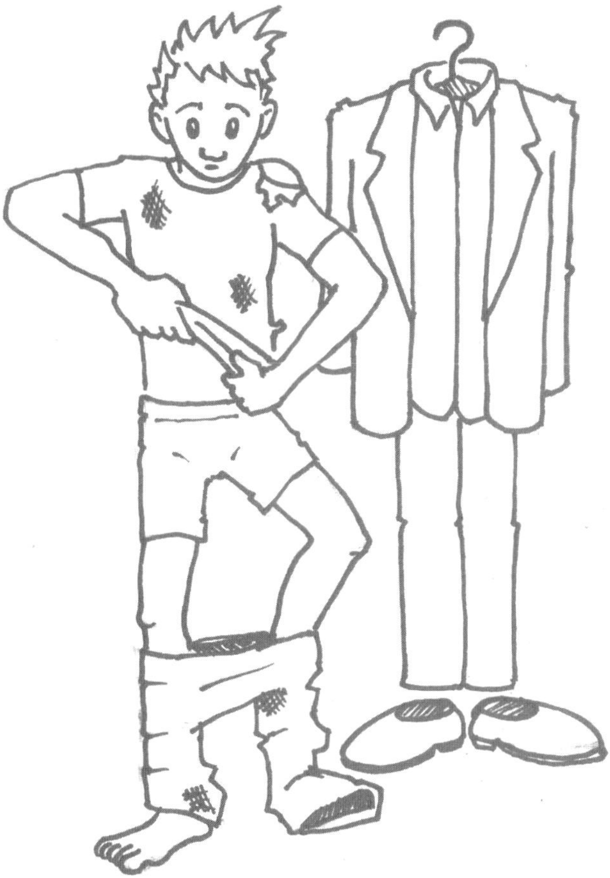

What if We Miss a Step?

1. **Surrendering to God's ways:**

If we miss surrendering to God's/love's ways, then we are still in the driver's seat, and where God needs to take charge to steer us in the right direction, we're still in His way!

2. **Metanoia — Spirit-led change of heart/mind:**

Where we still believe lies, we will stay "bound" in that area. When we ask God for help to show us what the truth really is, He will be loving in what He says. Anything unloving will not be of God. Believe the loving thought, no matter what your other thoughts say, and put your trust in this. As you do, your mind/heart changes and transformation becomes possible.

3. **Separating ourselves from lies, wrong beliefs, and actions:**

Where we don't peel away the old lies and behaviours, the new cannot come and become a part of us. (See Luke 5:33–38.)

Stuff that remains hidden and unsorted will fester and will come back later worse than when we put it away!

4. **Looking to God/love for truth and guidance:**

Where we are not trusting God to show us what to do, we are likely to repeat the same patterns of behaviour we've always known. God is keen to show us what ways are life-giving for us, no matter who we are and how many mistakes we've made. Take a chance and trust Him!

5. **Resisting the instant solutions:**

The Bible talks about laying aside our "lusts" — and it's not just talking about sexual issues! Our lusts are those things that we feel we want/need *now*, which we believe we cannot wait for.

The instant solutions are rarely the right ones, and instant gratification is not the doorway to wisdom. More likely it's the doorway to temptation to fix things ourselves, in our own strength, instead of relying on God's/love's guidance.

6. **Making life-embracing decisions:**

Knowing the right ways doesn't mean we automatically choose them. God will give us both the wisdom to know and the strength to do so. If we're not willing to trust God, we'll lose out.

Trust and Forgiveness

Someone once said to me, "I forgive, so I have to trust again."

Not necessarily.

Someone also once said to me, "I think I'm too forgiving."

I replied, "You can never be too forgiving."

What that person meant was "I'm too trusting."

They thought to forgive someone was to let them back into their life, let them do again the hurtful things that they've done to them. But if you keep giving them another chance and another chance and another chance, you're letting them walk all over you.

You need boundaries and wisdom. You can never forgive too much, but you can trust too much.

If someone has broken your trust, it takes time for it to rebuild, which can only happen bit by bit and also if we see them making a difference in their ways.

We need to be kind when people have shown an obvious remorse; some people do not say they're sorry, but you can tell they are by their actions.

Some people *can't* say the words because they think so little of themselves that it makes them feel so down to say they're sorry.

Some people don't know how to get an apology out, but the actions are the most important thing. Are their actions backing up the sense that they are sorry? Or do they repeat the offence?

Some of us do *need* to hear the words "I'm sorry," so it's important to encourage people to say so when they can.

Actions do speak louder than words here, as some people say they're sorry all the time and yet their actions never change. Cases like these may need protective boundaries to stop us getting hurt again and again.

Jesus said we should always forgive. If we stop forgiving, we start to let bitterness settle in.

Forgiveness is a lifetime decision; it's a lifestyle. You can't choose to be unforgiving with just one person and forgiving toward the rest. It can still eat you up on the inside.

The forgiveness we are shown by God is dependent on our ability to forgive others. "Forgive us our sins as we forgive those who sin against us." When Jesus said this he was saying "if you do not forgive each other's wrongs, your Father in heaven will not forgive yours."

We need to have the right kind of heart toward people. God has forgiven us so *much*. To withhold forgiveness and mercy from someone when we have received overflowing mercy and forgiveness from God would be wrong.

Chapter 7

Navigating the Landscape of Spiritual/Emotional Pain

We are not to live in reaction to the devil. We are to live in response to God.

~ Bill Johnson

I have a lovely card above my desk that says:

If you're going through hell, keep going.

~ Winston Churchill

This card has encouraged me from time to time that, on the other side of this trudge I'm in, there is hope. Sometimes life seems one long trudge. If that is where you are now, I am writing this for you!

However, nothing is as painful and heavy as the spiritual and emotional heaviness of hurt with unforgiveness. It stifles our soul.

I remember a dear lady called Dorothy whose husband and middle-aged daughter died in the same week. An awful situation. She was angry big-time with God, and I wasn't surprised.

I listened to her life story and had the privilege of her sharing her pain with me. Her pain was so great that I remember her telling me that she went to the local supermarket and wanted to scream at the top of her lungs, "I've lost my daughter and husband. How can you all just carry on with life as if nothing has happened?"

Hearing her story, it struck me that this poor lady had been robbed most of her life — by the one Jesus calls the "thief." What could I say in that situation that would make any difference whatsoever?

As I prayed about her I saw a picture of clouds all around her life, and I could relate to some of what she shared. For her, the sunshine didn't exist because it never shone on her, or so she felt.

I told her that I could see she had spent her whole life living under a cloud, but that I knew the sun existed and I wanted to take her to where the sun was.

Within a year Dorothy was much changed. She had forgiven God so much, and the healing that came with it meant that she and He were now best friends. She let go of the blame she felt toward God and herself, and started to discover a new joy and peace like she had not anticipated. A truly speedy and remarkable healing!

Ultimately, Dorothy saved herself by choosing to believe what God said rather than what the thief told her.

Battered or 'Boundaried?'

Boundaries are designed to protect those things that are precious — in this case, our hearts.

We should know about healthy boundaries from a very young age.

Some examples of boundaries:

- Speed limits,
- The law and police enforcing it, and
- Even door locks!

Healing can be hindered because we allow all kinds of things to happen to us by not having protective boundaries in place. We end up feeling tossed about, battered, and bruised, and anything good that we begin to grasp gets snatched from our hands before it can become established.

Boundaries are necessary to protect that which is valuable and precious, so that life can thrive, and that which can destroy, overrun, or distract us from life, is kept at bay.

Initially in a garden, we need to clear the weeds. We need to keep pests out — not just cats but also greenflies, slugs, and the birds that eat my strawberries!

There are all kinds of things we need to do that mark this garden as ours. If we want to grow a certain type of garden and we don't want everything we grow to be eaten by slugs or birds, we do things to protect parts of the garden — to create exactly what it is we're trying to create.

Unless we're willing to enforce those boundaries, to put slug pellets out, to put netting over our strawberries, or to put a gate on our garden to stop the cats from coming in, then our attempts will be weak and useless.

Any boundaries can be overcome unless we're willing to enforce them.

An example of a mild boundary when it comes to people would be: "When you do that, this happens, and I don't like the consequence, or it makes me feel down. Could you please avoid it?"

Or, more specifically: "Every time we speak, you interrupt me and I lose my train of thought. I'd really appreciate it if you could just wait until I've finished speaking so that I don't forget."

A firmer boundary would be: "If you keep doing____, then there will be a consequence. I will walk away, etc."

Or: "If you keep shouting at me/being unreasonable, I've made it very clear what the boundary is and what I will do as a consequence."

A strong boundary sometimes is needed.

There may be some very toxic relationships or critical people in our lives, or circumstances that will definitely sabotage our ability to succeed.

However, none of us should be heavy-handed when we don't need to be.

Walking out just because you're being interrupted might be an example of a firmer response than is actually needed, when simply saying something first may be sufficient.

Imprisoned by Feelings

Where we have strong negative feelings, it shows us the scars on our spirit — where we have been wounded, misunderstood, unjustly treated, abused, bullied, etc.

Sometimes we may have these strong negative feelings and not be aware of how they got there. Maybe we have had a good life so far and they just seem out of place.

We know that diseases can be inherited genetically. So can the health of our spirit — not always, but we can have a predisposition to certain things like low self-esteem, anger, unforgiveness, etc. from our families.

But take heart: God doesn't care how many issues you have. Why?

Because *you are not your issues*. You and your issues are separate.

As a wise person once said, "Your condition is not your position."

In other words, your condition may be battle-weary, sore, and grumpy (or any number of negative feelings), but your position as a saved and much-loved son or daughter of God is different.

The only real mistake is the one from which we learn nothing.
~John Powell

Letting Out the Pain

Sometimes pain needs to surface before we can recognise and process the underlying negative emotion. This is best done with one or two accountable others, not necessarily screaming in a public place, if you can help it! Most often I've just had a good cry to myself or with another — and once it is out, I have been able to talk about the cause of it with more objectivity.

You see, some people can think they're being healthy expressing their negative feelings, when really they're not interested in solving them. They're just interested in expressing them to others all the time, which doesn't help them, and it certainly doesn't help those who are subject to them! Going on a rampage of anger, abuse, etc. causes more damage, not less.

There's the classic story of when I spoke about anger: I asked a colleague, Tony, if I could "tear him off a strip" during my talk, and he said, "Sure."

So, I told everyone, "I'm glad to be here but had a pain parking because some thoughtless 'moron' decided to park in my place. And guess who that person was? Yes, you Tony!"

(All the time I was getting angrier, and more loud and abusive)

"How could you be so thoughtless? You knew I was coming today! You're always thoughtless. You don't think of others and I'm sick of it! Do you hear me? *Sick of it!!!!*"

Then I calmly turned to the audience and said, "So, how do you all feel about that?"

My mother, who happened to be visiting, said, "Flabbergasted!"

We laughed, and I got on with the job of explaining that anger that is allowed to rampage unchecked has a damaging effect on others.

Actually, I used to be a very angry person, but only a couple of times has God healed a hurt by allowing it to surface like that, and, thankfully, then it was when I was in a safe place.

Healing Tears

Tears are the best form of expressing hurt and healing. I find it easy.

Some people find it hard to cry; that's okay. My guess is that, when the time is right, God will bring them up.

If we find we have unwanted feelings coming up and it's not the right time to sort them (such as when we're at work or we don't want to hurt anyone), we can push them down for a time.

However, do your best not to forget about them, because sometimes feelings get past their "Best Before" date and come up with a vengeance, and we cannot control the way they surface then.

Where we have learnt to ignore our feelings altogether, our feelings can become hardened and seem like they're not there at all. This is because we've not loved ourselves enough to listen to ourselves and honour our pain (i.e., acknowledge it and treat it the way it should be treated). Don't ignore your emotions; listen to them. They may not be objective truth, but they are valid and will be telling you something you need to know and may need to take account of.

It is a dangerous thing to turn our feelings off altogether and not process them. That is when real damage can happen to our mental health, and we ignore our hearts at our expense.

Tears are words the heart can't express. ~ Unknown

No Fear?

Don't worry about anything; instead, pray about everything. Tell God what you need, and thank him for all he has done.
~ Philippians 4:6

Most of us know we shouldn't worry. But we do.

Most of us know we shouldn't have stress. But it's hard.

Many of us recognise that when we're fearful we can make the wrong decisions. Fear is often entwined with unforgiveness, so it's worth looking at this a bit more, as we will have to face certain fears as we learn to forgive and let go of some things.

Fear also comes because we don't feel secure or that God is with us, or because we've lost sight of Him.

Recognising Fear in Ourselves

- An over-anxiety, stress
- A tenseness, a knot in the stomach
- An aversion to certain people/situations
- Fear over a few issues or many
- A lack of trust
- Paranoia (Is this person/people against me?)
- Dread

Where Does Fear Come From?

It comes because we believed at some point that we were not fully loved, protected, or valued.

People who know they're fully loved, fully secure, and protected do not fear where they don't need to.

There is no fear in love; but perfect love casts out fear, because fear involves torment. But he who fears has not been made perfect in love.

~ I John 4:18

(In other words, the more truly loved we become, the more fear will fall away.)

How Can Fear Affect Us?

(This list is not complete, and I've included biblical references for those of you who would like them.)

1. **Fear paralyses us:**
   An inability to act for fear of getting it wrong or being hurt. *(Job 31:33–35)*

2. **Fear can cause us to hate:**
Fear of man when combined with unforgiveness produces hate further down the line. *(1 Samuel 18:27–29)*

3. **Fear can make God look like He is not in control and makes our enemy out to be bigger than he really is:**
We often feel compelled to take action against a person without knowing that it is the right thing to do.

4. **Fear causes us to stop trusting:**
Not being able to trust someone if we believe them to be responsible for a past hurt, or not trusting people in the future because trusting people in the past has gotten you hurt. *(Proverbs 29:25 NKJV)*

5. **Fear of people becomes part of us instead of God pleasing:** Doing the wrong thing because of pressure from others. *(1 Samuel 15:23–25 NKJV)*

6. **Fear leads us astray from God's ways.**
(2 Kings 17:6–8 NKJV)

7. **Fear causes our courage to disappear!**
(Judges 6:26–28 NKJV)

8. **Fear makes us try to control others.**
(1 Samuel 13:18–20 NLT; Leviticus 25:42–44 NKJV)

9. **Fear causes confusion.**
(Exodus 23:26–28 NKJV)

10. **Fear causes us to lose hope.**
(Psalm 143:3–5 NLT)

11. **Fear stops us from loving truth.**
(Proverbs 1:28–30 NLT)

God and Justice: Letting Go, or Letting God?

We must develop and maintain the capacity to forgive. He who is devoid of the power to forgive is devoid of the power to love. There is some good in the worst of us and some evil in the best of us. When we discover this, we are less prone to hate our enemies.

~ Martin Luther King, Jr.

What to Do with the Pain of Injustice

Jesus speaks clearly in the Gospels about the seemingly extreme measures we're to take in forgiving. It could seem like He has a bias toward those who have done wrong or that He doesn't fully understand the pain that is caused by another person's wrongdoing. Those of us who know Jesus are clear that is not the case. Look at the Gospels of Matthew, Mark, Luke, and John yourself if you want to check them out.

If we're truthful, most of us want to be able to forgive and let go; we just don't know how to do it, or sometimes if it is the "right" thing to do. Who will see justice is done if we forgive? What do you do with the grot that you're left with that they caused?

Tainted by Vengeance

The Old Testament says "an eye for an eye, a tooth for a tooth." There's that sense that if someone's done you wrong, you have the right to pay him back for it. However, Gandhi once said, "An eye for an eye and a tooth for a tooth and the whole world would soon be blind and toothless." There's truth in that.

If we go by the Old Testament's philosophy, we think it's okay to have vengeance in our hearts, but if we do, it's hard to also take Jesus' love on board. We'll be tainted by vengeance.

So when Jesus came along and said things like "love your enemy," it was quite revolutionary.

Vengeance (us wanting payback ourselves) stops us from being like Jesus, because Jesus didn't pay people back for everything they did wrong. He was forgiving and tried to identify people's mistakes clearly to see what their motive really was.

The story of the woman caught in adultery is a good example, and it also allowed Jesus to confront the Pharisees and say, "If you think you haven't got any sin, feel free to throw the first stone" *(John 8:1–11).*

So, the thing about God and justice in the New Testament is about repentance. Is the person sorry? If people are sorry and they are trying to improve and make up for their mistakes, it is our responsibility to forgive them.

The Best Avenger

Other people can be simply blind to their mistakes and weaknesses, but we don't always have to confront them and especially don't have to punish them. We should give the justice up to God. "Vengeance is *mine*" said God. "*I* will repay" *(Romans 12:18–20)*.

In other words, leave it to God because God knows what's true, and where people really are doing wrong things. Eventually we will all be standing before God, and we will all be judged.

The problem with that is that if someone said he made a mistake, you can't tell what is in his heart (i.e., if he is telling the truth). Only God can do that.

...for the LORD searches all hearts and understands all the intent of the thoughts. ~ 1 Chronicles 28:9

In the Bible when people were going to be put out of the city or stoned to death, there was actually a place, a town, where they could go to live instead. They didn't actually die; God had that allowance for His people if, for example, they killed someone by accident. God recognised that people make mistakes.

We need to trust God to apply justice where either we cannot apply it, because we don't know the facts, we don't know their hearts, we don't know their background, etc., or where we should not apply it, which includes the areas where we still have "live" emotion, because we may give them a harsher sentence. We need to be able to give those things to God.

In every way that I have thrown myself entirely onto God, He has been unfailingly faithful, He's been full of grace, and He's redeemed the situation way beyond what I could have done.

We need to be able to give up those situations to God, because then we can continue on with our lives and our healing. God has a particular heart for widows, orphans, and the poor (i.e., those who are on their own).

You shall not afflict any widow or fatherless child.

~ Exodus 22:22

If we are fatherless, are motherless, or don't have much, God has a special bias toward us and we can therefore trust Him even more to let go of things and to supply what we need. If we think we don't need God, we're not going to lean on Him and we're not going to receive His help.

Well, God is a God of justice, and, whilst we might want to be the one who takes "an eye for an eye a tooth for a tooth," we can't always act justly with hurt and sometimes hate in our heart.

There are strong laws in the Old Testament that mean that the person who sinned had severe consequences. I see a correlation between the Old Testament and the New Testament, but have come to the conclusion that sin ultimately involves some kind of rebellion against God's ways, whether or not we know it.

In the Old Testament we see judgment happened quickly, but in the New Testament we see that "mercy triumphs over judgment." Why the difference?

Well, the Old Testament laws, I believe, reflect spiritually what takes place when one person hurts another, himself, or God. He becomes constrained and spiritually blind, and ultimately he spiritually dies.

God can be trusted with overall judgment because, ultimately, only He can see into our hearts and know our thoughts and motives. He knows when we are wrongly accused, abused, and used, and will fight justice for us with the passion of a heroic lover, as we put ourselves into His hands.

Love for the Enemy

The love for equals is a human thing — of friend for friend, brother for brother. It is to love what is loving and lovely. The world smiles.

The love for the less fortunate is a beautiful thing — the love for those who suffer, for those who are poor, the sick, the failures, the unlovely. This is compassion, and it touches the heart of the world.

The love for the more fortunate is a rare thing — to love those who succeed where we fail, to rejoice without envy with those who rejoice, the love of the poor for the rich, of the black man for the white man. The world is always bewildered by its saints.

And then there is the love for the enemy — love for the one who does not love you but mocks, threatens, and inflicts pain. The tortured's love for the torturer. This is God's love.

It conquers the world.

God's Upside-Down World

God is love, and, if we're being restored to be like Him, then we need to know what is possible and not possible with God.

True love and hating people do not coexist: God doesn't hate people, just the things that we do that hurt ourselves, others, or Him.

Indeed, God feels great sorrow for those who have lost their way. He longs that all people would turn to Him and be made whole. This is why there are so many passages about love and actions in the Bible. True love that has been refined, does not hate. Same with vengeance, resentment, bitterness, etc.

The presence of these smellies keeps love at bay. For our own sake as well as others, we need to them go.

What we give to God entirely (where we die to self), God can fully redeem. Jesus talked about people hanging onto things for dear life and not realizing that the way to keep something is to let it go ...to God. A hurtful injustice given to God can be amazingly transformed!

I have so many stories to tell of myself and others on this front, but it all starts with giving the whole situation/ person to God and keeping our hands off.

Not just doing it for the result, though! Giving it to God because you trust Him ultimately to do the best for you.

And He said to all, If any person wills to come after Me, let him deny himself [disown himself, forget, lose sight of himself and his own interests, refuse and give up himself] and take up his cross daily and follow Me [cleave steadfastly to Me, conform wholly to My example in living and, if need be, in dying also].

~ Luke 9:23 Amplified Bible

What lies behind us and what lies before us are tiny matters compared to what lies within us.

~ Ralph Waldo Emerson

Chapter 8

Starting Afresh

New Creation

When we come to Christ, and we really give our all to God and we say "your way, not mine," then we die to ourselves and re-creation happens.

Many people want to scrap what's happened to them in life. They say they want to "start a new chapter" or "turn over a new leaf," but with God, what happens is more like starting a different book altogether.

When we follow God's ways through Jesus, we are given a brand new life, and we become re-created in it. The old has gone, the new has come.

Out with the Old, In with the New

The new stuff is like what we're planting in a freshly dug garden, with nothing planted in it. Jesus used an analogy of putting new wine in an old wineskin: You don't do it, because it affects the flavour.

Likewise, if we're planting new habits, all of our old stuff needs to be out, or we need to be in the process of chucking it out.

Then the way we plant this new stuff in our lives is by musing. Musing in lots of different ways in order to get this new life-giving stuff really rooted!

Getting the "New" Rooted: Attitude

Musing is not a modern concept. It's pondering but in a prayerful way — deep meditative thought on a deep level about things we don't often share with other people. We can choose to muse on good stuff or bad stuff, stuff that is life-giving or death-giving.

When the Israelites left Egypt, they were promised new land.

How many of them made it to the Promised Land? None, except Joshua and Caleb, and the children that were born in the wilderness.

The rest of the generation died because of what they mused on. They could not stop grumbling, complaining, getting distracted, and turning away from God. Only those few made it.

Because the Israelites moaned so much and showed how little they trusted God, they didn't inherit the promises. They were withheld from them *by their own actions* because they were feeding negativity and doubt, and given to their children instead.

Even Caleb had a wobbly when he saw the giants in the land, but Aaron said, "No, we can do it. We can take them."

We need to remember that what we feed, grows — including fear! Likewise, what we choose to muse on will produce life or produce death, emotionally, spiritually, etc.

Getting the "New" Rooted: Inviting

In the fresh garden of our heart and mind, we're welcoming the Holy Spirit on a daily basis. People like Benny Hinn wake up and say "Good morning, Holy Spirit!", like He's just there, which He is. He sees God as the personality He is. We should be welcoming the Holy Spirit.

If we don't know God, we say, "Good morning, Spirit of Love!"

And the Holy Spirit will pick up on that, because God is love. It's one of His other names, so it's not a major problem!

Getting the "New" Rooted: Discovering

Another way we prepare to plant new things is that we discover the many treasures that are written for us in the Bible — all the promises, encouragements, and support. So many of us haven't discovered them for ourselves, and we could do with reading them and knowing them. The Holy Spirit can't put those in us; *we* need to read them.

Getting the "New" Rooted: Reflecting on Personal Words

Some of us have been blessed enough to receive prophetic words (encouraging words from God) on our journey.

I remember when my first husband left. Someone said to me that God told her that "clipped wings will fly again." I felt like my wings had been clipped. Someone else gave me a picture: "Out of the ashes, a rose bush will grow." Those were the things I held on to in the difficult times, so when God started to re-create things, I thought "Wow, I *am* starting to fly again. God is using this stuff to bring beauty after all."

From "Mush" to Miracle

Look at St. Paul: He murdered Christians and persecuted the innocent, and yet God could turn his heart.

The reason God was able to turn Paul's heart is because Paul, after his experience speaking with Jesus, recognised the state of it and was then open to God's lead and to transformation.

When we're being transformed, there's that horrible stage in-between where we turn into mushy primeval gunge! When a caterpillar is in its cocoon, it literally dies as a caterpillar, disintegrates into mush (but life-giving, nutrient-filled mush!), and after time becomes re-created into a beautiful butterfly. It's not like the caterpillar just sprouts butterfly wings; it becomes a completely different thing.

When God brings healing in us — and forgiving *is* healing — we go from being broken to being whole. We don't get "fixed," but whole, as in strong. We go from being the victim to being victorious. We go from being ignorant to having insight. *That's* the kind of transformation God does as we give up our way and ask for His guidance.

As we apply divine truth to our lives, we really are set free.

Keeping Focused on the Key Things

Seeing the path you need to take, and getting on it and staying on it, can be dependent on a number of things.

If we struggle with low self-esteem, have a lot of accusation in our lives, or are not very good at forgiving ourselves, etc., we need to remember that Jesus' sacrifice for us was sufficient: We don't need to do anything more!

We'll want to try to make it up to God and please Him in other ways, but that's getting into the old religious way of doing things.

God wants a relationship, not religion. All relationship, no religion.

You see, Jesus saw the "religious" as simply going through the motions.

Being friends with Jesus is the closest relationship we can have with anybody.

Anything else that gets in the way of God is what the Bible calls an "idol."

God knows we are at our best when our eyes are focused on Him because that's what we were created for. When we look at Him, we discover ourselves more fully. We see the love for us on His face, and, when we see how much God loves us, it transforms us and makes us see ourselves even better.

We're Covered!

I spent quite a while musing on Colossians 3 because the Holy Spirit kept drawing me there. At the time I had no idea why, but I read it every day for over a month because the Holy Spirit was drawing me there. Slowly, it filled in blanks for me, showing me that it wasn't just my shortcomings that Jesus died for. Even when I felt I failed because I wasn't as strong as I wanted to be, He covers me (and all of us) well enough so that, whatever accusations come our way, we can say "I'm covered." A bit like insurance cover, we're covered by Jesus: "I'm with Jesus Christ Mutual Life."

We don't need to feel any sense of shame as long as what we're doing on a regular basis is taking our stuff, giving it to Jesus, and having that relationship with Him where we're exchanging our crap for His goodness.

As long as that is happening, shame is not meant to be part of the process.

Condemnation is not part of the process.

Self- judgment is not part of the process.

Accusation is not part of the process.

Criticism is not part of the process.

Rejection is not part of the process; we are not rejected by God.

He thinks we're amazing.

Rejection is a lie that comes straight from the enemy. Sometimes we feel rejection very strongly, but what we're actually feeling is the enemy's rejection in us. We are never rejected by God.

Some things we feel, like rejection, are very strong, and therefore we feel like we own it. We don't, because we are not actually rejected. Even if we're really close to God, we can feel rejection but mustn't listen to it because we can trust Him.

Relationship and Identity

Once we have this relationship with God, we fully understand that we're His children, and we begin to grow into the people we were created to be.

Everything that's His, we're meant to inherit.

God has a father's heart for His children. He wants us to be the best we can be. He loves and affirms for who we are, not what we do, and the closer we get to Him, the more like Him we become.

Not only are we sons of the Father, but we're also part of the bride of Christ, which is a different kind of love. We're loved in two very distinct but very profound ways.

The Enemy can deceive us into forgetting what our identity is, and we can waste most of our life because we don't know who we are.

If we knew who we are and what God has put at our disposal, we would never be sad, we wouldn't have unforgiveness, we wouldn't have bitterness, and we wouldn't feel rejected.

Jesus is our bridegroom; God is our father. How can we not feel loved? The more we understand this and feel His love, the more we fulfil our potential and gain fullness of life.

Chapter 9

Transforming the Foundation

When the Holy Spirit is in you, it is illegal not to conquer something.

~ Bill Johnson

Food for thought.

The Holy Spirit is given to us so that we can be overcomers. I'd like to end this book with some reminders:

- Remaining de-cluttered means nipping things in the bud.
- Recognise that wholeness is a journey.
- Focus on the positive as we move forward.

Remaining De-Cluttered Means Nipping Things in the Bud

It's very easy to get cluttered again, after you've already de-cluttered.

One of the phrases I use in my household for tidying is "return to ready" — in other words, try to put something back in the state it should be in order to be ready for use. So a dirty mug that's been left in the lounge goes into the kitchen and gets washed, dried, and put back in the cupboard. That's "return to ready." Dirty washing isn't just put in the laundry basket; it's washed, it's dried, it's hung up/ironed, it's put back in the wardrobe. *Then* it's returned to ready.

The way we keep our spirits at a "return to ready" stage is by nipping things in the bud; wherever possible, we nab the little "weeds" as quickly as we can. We don't leave them to fester. We carry out Matthew 18 and keep communication as strong as possible. Many issues boil down to communication, because it gets confused and distorted by people's issues, so it's important we keep this clear. One of the things Matthew 18 does is give you the opportunity to go and talk to someone, clear up the communication and hopefully nip things in the bud.

Another way to keep the past de-cluttered is to delete offence from our person. We can do this by *choosing not to get offended*. This is actually simpler than it sounds. In order to do this we just have to assume ignorance of others for their actions, not assume and attach a motive to it. It's easier to forgive a mistake than a deliberate offence. We can't possibly know people's motives; if we point a finger at another, there's three pointing back at us. It's always best to assume people's ignorance, because 95% of the time that will be the case.

We need to separate the sin from the sinner.

Jesus said, "Forgive them (the people), for they know not what they do (the issue)."

We need to do the same: to recognise that people do things without recognising the full consequences of what they do. If we separate the sin from the sinner, we can still not like something that someone does, yet still like that person and have good feelings towards him or her.

Another way to get de-cluttered is to **recognise the "smellies"** (unhealthy thoughts, emotions. and habits) a mile off and learn to deal with them before they arrive.

These things *do* come our way. There *will* be times when we get angry, there *will* be times when we misunderstand, there likely *will* be times that we get offended, but the quicker we can get over these things and deal with them, the better.

If you think you think these things are never going to come knocking again once you've dealt with them, then you're mistaken, because they will. We just have to be ready to deal with them when they do. We mustn't put it off; we must nab those weeds in the bud.

Recognise that Wholeness Is a Journey

We're journeying from our old selves to becoming new beings, with different thoughts, behaviours, and actions.

We need to ditch the past behaviour that we have — e.g. I always used to say "I never..." but I'm very careful about the language I use these days, because I recognise that words can be binding. They can write our destiny, so we need to be very careful that our language is representative of what we truly mean. If we find we do say something that we shouldn't, we need to take it back and rectify it as soon as possible.

The way we keep planting new habits is by focusing on God, as I've said in the previous chapter. The way we think about the things of God is to celebrate things that are in the present that we're grateful for and to look at how far we've come, even if it's only been a day. We need to praise God and ourselves for progress and thank God for giving us the strength for a new day. The Bible says "the steadfast love of the LORD never ceases; his mercy has never come to an end, it is new every morning." (Lamentations 3:22-24) God's love and mercies are present with us now, and it's up to us whether we want to take advantage of that.

Another way we focus on things of God is by feeding ourselves on testimonies. If we want to overcome, then the stories of those that have overcome are inspiring and encouraging; these are real spiritual manna! We hear of people taking positive action, and we need to celebrate with them, because we may be not long behind them!

We have to keep on cherishing. Cherishing has to be a lifestyle. It's when we're not feeling loved and supported that it's easy for the enemy to get us down, distract us, distort communication, and throw stuff at us that we can't handle. We need to keep up a cherishing lifestyle; it will keep us God-centred and keep our enemy out.

We also need to keep acting on the "rhema" word: **God's living and active word to us.** This may be from the Bible (from the "logos") if it seems highlighted to us, or it may just be something that the Holy Spirit is telling us that day. (Just to be clear, it will never conflict with the overall essence of the Bible.)

We need to keep acting on the "rhema" word because, where we take information in, we hear a thought and we don't act on it, we're stopping the flow of the Holy Spirit in us. We need to act on it if we want God to keep talking to us more and more.

Another way to focus on the things of God is to use 1 Corinthians 13 as a guide. It's so helpful to muse upon 1 Corinthians 13. Musing on those things that God highlights — pondering prayerfully, reflecting, or whatever you want to call it — they're the things to keep up.

Recognise when we're going into a difficult time that it's not necessarily how we're going to feel in an hour, a day, a month, or a year. As we look to the future, let's remember the grace, love, and mercy we have been shown because it's also for the present, to affect our actions, both now and in the future. We mustn't be like the unforgiving servant, not allowing God's love and generosity in the present to affect the rest of our life.

If we keep our eyes fixed on Jesus, which the Bible says is what perfects our faith, He will guide us in whatever way we need. He already has our future in His hands, because God's outside time. As we continue to seek truth and become a lifetime seeker of truth and love, then we will find that God is there.

We cannot hold unforgiveness in the human heart without it detrimentally affecting the way we see and react to life. Our hearts, our health and our holiness are at stake.

Pursuing forgiveness is part of learning to love ourselves, others and God and ultimately makes us the person we were designed to be.

To forgive is to set a prisoner free and discover the prisoner was YOU.

~ *Unknown*

If it's greater freedom wholeness and love you want, check out the free resources at www.lovef1rst.com.